JOURNEYS

Reader's Notebook

Student Edition

Grade 6

Houghton Mifflin Harcourt

Contents

Unit 4

Unit 5

Unit 6

The School Story

Write a Book Review

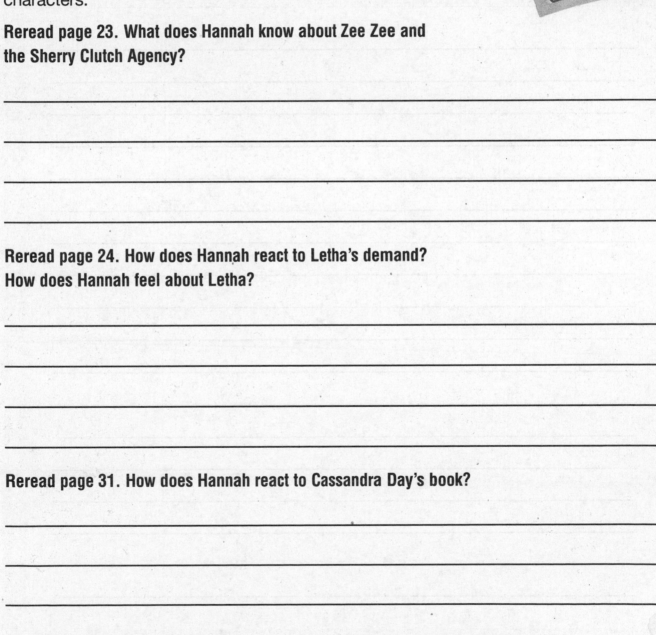

Natalie's mother, Hannah, must write an initial review for "The Cheater" for her boss, Letha. Use text evidence to answer the questions that describe Hannah's feelings about the other characters.

Reread page 23. What does Hannah know about Zee Zee and the Sherry Clutch Agency?

_____

_____

_____

_____

Reread page 24. How does Hannah react to Letha's demand? How does Hannah feel about Letha?

_____

_____

_____

_____

Reread page 31. How does Hannah react to Cassandra Day's book?

_____

_____

_____

_____

In an e-mail, write an initial review of "The Cheater" for Letha, Hannah's boss. Describe the author and the book and tell why the book should or should not be published.

New Message
To: **Letha**
From: **Hannah**
Subject: **Review of "The Cheater" by Cassandra Day**

_____

_____

_____

_____

_____

_____

_____

_____

_____

_____

_____

_____

_____

_____

_____

_____

_____

Prefixes *dis-*, *ex-*, *inter-*, *non-*

The words in the box begin with the prefixes *dis-* or *non-*, meaning "not"; *ex-*, meaning "out" or "beyond"; or *inter-*, meaning "between/among." Choose the word that best completes each sentence.

disappeared	nonstop	displease	displace	exceed
nonfiction	extract	interact	interlace	interview

1. The rabbit _____ into the bushes.

2. The dentist had to _____ the rotten tooth.

3. Put a few large rocks in the birdbath to _____ some water.

4. Do not _____ the boundary of the playground during recess.

5. Talking during the assembly will _____ the speaker.

6. Being at the amusement park all day was _____ fun.

7. Reporters like to _____ famous people for the news.

8. A good _____ book sticks to the facts.

9. The designer wanted to _____ the cloth with gold silk thread.

10. When good friends _____, they feel relaxed and natural.

Short Vowels

Basic Complete the puzzle by writing the Basic Word for each clue.

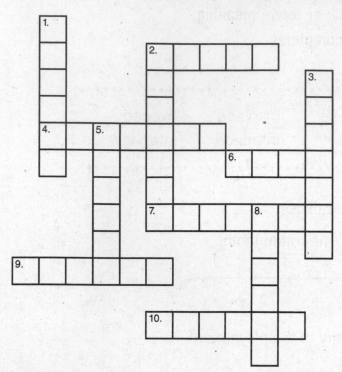

Spelling Words

1. batch
2. reject
3. vanish
4. sloppy
5. rhythm
6. blunder
7. strict
8. meadow
9. recover
10. cleanse
11. text
12. mystery
13. expand
14. bluff
15. promptly
16. initials
17. statue
18. polish
19. somehow
20. dreadful

Challenge

salary
quintet
magnetic
tepid
intact

Across

2. a group of something
4. to make clean
6. a book or other piece of writing
7. to return to a normal condition
9. a grassy field
10. to make smooth and shiny

Down

1. enforced all the time
2. a mistake
3. something that is not understood
5. become larger
8. disappear

Challenge How could you earn money to buy a bike? Write sentences with your ideas. Use three of the Challenge Words. Write on a separate sheet of paper.

Spelling Word Sort

Write each Basic Word beside the correct heading.

/ă/ spelled *a*	
/ĕ/ spelled *e* or *ea*	
/ĭ/ spelled *i* or *y*	
/ŏ/ spelled *o*	
/ŭ/ spelled *u* or *o*-consonant-*e*	

Spelling Words

1. batch
2. reject
3. vanish
4. sloppy
5. rhythm
6. blunder
7. strict
8. meadow
9. recover
10. cleanse
11. text
12. mystery
13. expand
14. bluff
15. promptly
16. initials
17. statue
18. polish
19. somehow
20. dreadful

Challenge
salary
quintet
magnetic
tepid
intact

Challenge Add the Challenge Words to your Word Sort. Some words will fit in more than one group.

Connect to Reading Look through *The School Story*. Find words in the selection that have the /ă/, /ĕ/, /ĭ/, /ŏ/, and /ŭ/ spelling patterns on this page. Add them to your Word Sort.

Proofreading for Spelling

Find the misspelled words and circle them. Write them correctly on the lines below.

The author's work was sloopy, and the writing was pretty dredfull. There was no rhythim or style to the writing. The mistery the author tried to create didn't work. As a publisher, Martin could never print the tex .

Yet Martin felt very uneasy, somhow, after he promply wrote the note to rejeckt the writer's story once again. Martin glanced out the window. What he saw there made him feel that he might have made a blundar.

A young man was standing like a statew, staring intently up at his office. The man's stare was not a bluf because Martin could see the hopefulness in the man's face. Martin decided that if the writer was truly dedicated, he could allow him one last chance to pollesh his work.

Spelling Words

1. batch
2. reject
3. vanish
4. sloppy
5. rhythm
6. blunder
7. strict
8. meadow
9. recover
10. cleanse
11. text
12. mystery
13. expand
14. bluff
15. promptly
16. initials
17. statue
18. polish
19. somehow
20. dreadful

1. _____   7. _____
2. _____   8. _____
3. _____   9. _____
4. _____   10. _____
5. _____   11. _____
6. _____   12. _____

Subjects and Predicates

A **sentence** is a group of words that expresses a complete thought. All sentences have two parts: a subject and a predicate. The **simple subject** of a sentence is whom or what the sentence is about. The **simple predicate** is the main word that describes the action or the state of being. The **simple predicate** is a verb.

Thinking Questions
Which part of the sentence tells whom or what the sentence is about? Which part describes the action or state of being?

   subject predicate
The author placed her book on the shelf.

Activity Underline the simple subject in the sentences. Circle the simple predicate.

1. Carla opened the manuscript.

2. The proofreader checked all the spelling.

3. Before lunch, she finished the chapter.

4. The publisher told him to make the changes.

5. The index is the last part of the book.

6. The editor called right before dinner.

7. Shannon helped Carla with the writing.

8. The author finally felt comfortable with all the edits.

Complete Subjects and Predicates

A **complete subject** tells whom or what a sentence is about, including any words that modify it.

A **complete predicate** tells what the complete subject is or does. It includes a verb or verbs and any words that modify them.

complete subject   complete predicate
A box of cookies landed on my desk.

Thinking Questions
Which part of this sentence tells whom or what the sentence is about? Which part of this sentence includes the verb and any words that modify it?

Activity Circle the complete subject in each sentence. Underline the complete predicate.

1. People in publishing know about correct punctuation.

2. Great authors write with their readers in mind.

3. The publisher sent the editor a text message.

4. Some authors write non-fiction books.

5. A young, unknown writer sent in a long manuscript.

6. Confused readers may want to review the footnotes.

7. The printing company is waiting for the pages.

8. Science fiction is my favorite type of book.

Fragments and Run-ons

A **sentence fragment** is a group of words that does not express a complete thought. A **run-on sentence** is two or more sentences run together with commas or without punctuation.

sentence fragment	**complete sentence**
A dance on Saturday.	A dance will be held on Saturday.

run-on sentence

A dance will be held on Saturday, I'm going.

complete sentence

A dance will be held on Saturday, and I'm going.

Thinking Questions
Does the group of words express a complete thought? Is the sentence made of two sentences with commas or without punctuation?

Activity Label each group of words *sentence fragment*, *run-on sentence*, or *complete sentence*. Correct any sentence fragments or run-on sentences.

1. Manuscript to the publisher. _____

_____

2. The author read the final pages she was happy. _____

_____

3. Three editors in the company from California. _____

_____

4. The proofreader gave the corrections to the writer. _____

_____

5. Meetings with the publisher on Tuesdays and Thursdays. _____

_____

6. Mr. Brown is president of the publishing company, he works hard. _____

_____

Contractions

Incorrect	**Hasn't no** one read the story?
Correct	**Hasn't anyone** read the story?
Incorrect	She printed copies for us, and **there** on the table.
Correct	She printed copies for us, and **they're** on the table.

1–6. **Write the correct word in parentheses to complete the sentence.**

1. I _____ had no time to read it. **(have, haven't)**

2. His manuscripts don't _____ require changes. **(ever, never)**

3. Footnotes are important, so be sure you haven't left _____ out. **(any, none)**

4. _____ hard to believe the book is going to be published. **(Its, It's)**

5. I think that _____ writing an interesting story. **(you're, your)**

6. _____ are good chapters in the book's middle section. **(They're, There)**

7–10. **The rules below have errors. Circle the error. Then write the correct word on the line.**

7. Don't keep food or drinks nowhere near the manuscript.

_____

8. Nothing from the proofreader shouldn't be included in the manuscript. _____

9. Save your edits often if your working on an important file.

_____

10. Be respectful to authors. There the ones who provide the original stories. _____

Connect to Writing

Sentence Fragment	The mother and baby elephant at the zoo.
Complete Sentence	The mother and baby elephant live at the zoo.
Run-on Sentence	Danielle gave me a book to read, I finished it in one night.
Complete Sentence	Danielle gave me a book to read, and I finished it in one night.

Read the sentences. Fix sentence fragments and run-on sentences to form complete sentences. Write the new sentences on the lines.

1. The manuscript is long, we can't reduce its length.

   _____

   _____

2. The new writer learned a lot, she received the editor's comments.

   _____

   _____

3. The final pages delivered to the printing company yesterday.

   _____

   _____

4. He edits with a red pen, I prefer blue.

   _____

   _____

5. Several chapters rewritten by the author.

   _____

   _____

6. The printing company should always be notified by five o'clock, that is when they close.

   _____

   _____

Focus Trait: Development
Using Precise Words and Descriptive Details to Reveal Characters

Sentence with Basic Facts	Sentence That Reveals the Character
Mark could not find his manuscript.	Mark felt a sense of panic as he searched frantically for his missing manuscript.

Revise these sentences to reveal the characters' thoughts, feelings, and actions. Include precise words and descriptive details.

Sentence with Basic Facts	Sentence That Reveals the Character
1. Mark spent weeks writing his manuscript.	
2. When Mark let me read his story, he was nervous.	
3. I smiled as I read the story.	
4. I was happy for my friend.	

Name _____ Date _____

Lesson 2
READER'S NOTEBOOK

Knots in
My Yo-Yo String
Independent Reading

Reader's Guide

Knots in My Yo-Yo String

The Feeling of Writing

Jerry Spinelli wrote *Knots in My Yo-Yo String* to explain why he became a writer. Reread portions of the text to learn how Spinelli feels about these experiences.

Reread page 53. What words or phrases does Spinelli use that show how he feels before he writes the poem "Goal to Go"?

_____

_____

_____

Reread page 57. Spinelli explains his early writing experiences. What clues in the text show how Spinelli may have felt about these experiences?

_____

_____

_____

Reread page 58. What details in the text provide clues about Spinelli's feelings about the chicken-culprit story?

_____

_____

_____

Imagine that you are Jerry Spinelli, writing in your journal about how you felt during each episode. Extend what is in the text by describing your feelings.

After the Football Game

_____

_____

_____

_____

_____

Early Writing Experiences

_____

_____

_____

_____

_____

Chicken-Culprit Story

_____

_____

_____

_____

Suffixes -er, -or, -ar, -ist, -ian, -ent

Knots in My Yo-yo String
Vocabulary Strategies:
Suffixes -er, -or, -ar, -ist, -ian, -ent

The words in the box end with a suffix that means "someone who." Choose the word that best completes each sentence.

| respondent | recipient | popular | printer | reporter |
| investigator | mentor | violinist | scientist | librarian |

1. Not every _____ had answered all of the survey questions.

2. The _____ performed his recital piece with no mistakes.

3. Every third-grade student was assigned a sixth-grade _____ .

4. She asked the _____ for help finding a book for her research report.

5. Write the name of the _____ on the outside of the envelope.

6. The famous singer is _____ with people of all ages.

7. They took the flyers to the _____ so they could give copies to all of their friends.

8. An _____ was called to the scene of the factory accident.

9. If you like working in a lab, you might want to be a _____ .

10. Lauren wanted to be a _____ because she loved watching the news.

Long Vowels

Basic Write the Basic Word that belongs in each group.

1. necklace, earrings, _____

2. unspeaking, silent, _____

3. hide, cover, _____

4. urge, persuade, _____

5. trust, depend, _____

6. harm, mistreat, _____

7. erase, remove, _____

8. commit, dedicate, _____

9. loyal, constant, _____

10. cage, enclose, _____

11. triumph, prosper, _____

Challenge Write a persuasive letter to your local government that supports the funding of a local animal shelter. Use three of the Challenge Words. Write on a separate sheet of paper.

Spelling Words

1. scene
2. bracelet
3. mute
4. strive
5. faithful
6. devote
7. rhyme
8. succeed
9. coax
10. rely
11. conceal
12. forgave
13. lonesome
14. delete
15. confine
16. exceed
17. terrain
18. reproach
19. abuse
20. defeat

Challenge
ratify
serene
refute
appraise
humane

Name _____ Date _____

Spelling Word Sort

Write each Basic Word beside the correct heading.

/ā/ spelled *a*-consonant-*e* or *ai*	
/ē/ spelled *e*-consonant-*e*, *ea*, or *ee*	
/ī/ spelled *i*-consonant-*e*, *y*-consonant-*e* or *y*	
/ō/ spelled *o*-consonant-*e* or *oa*	
/ū/ spelled *u*-consonant-*e*	

Spelling Words

1. scene
2. bracelet
3. mute
4. strive
5. faithful
6. devote
7. rhyme
8. succeed
9. coax
10. rely
11. conceal
12. forgave
13. lonesome
14. delete
15. confine
16. exceed
17. terrain
18. reproach
19. abuse
20. defeat

Challenge
ratify
serene
refute
appraise
humane

Challenge Add the Challenge Words to your Word Sort.

Connect to Reading Look through *Knots in My Yo-yo String*. Find words in the selection that have the /ā/, /ē/, /ī/, /ō/, and /ū/ spelling patterns on this page. Add them to your Word Sort.

Proofreading for Spelling

Find the misspelled words and circle them. Write them correctly on the lines below.

Lucy was happy that she had managed to coxe her mother into letting her wear her mother's new braclet to the movies. Then she lost it.

When Lucy got home, her mother asked her if she had a good time. Lucy was mutte. She was afraid of her mother's reproch. She didn't know how to tell her mother, so Lucy tried to conseal her empty wrist behind her back.

Lucy didn't succeed. Her faithfull mother went over to Lucy and asked her again if she had a good time. Lucy had to relie on quick thinking. She shoved her hand in her pocket. "It was fun," she said, then turned and headed upstairs. "I have to devot some time to studying. I need to strife for better grades."

Her mother narrowed her eyes. "Really?" As Lucy climbed the stairs, she called, "I need my bracelet back, please."

Lucy accepted defeat. Thankfully, her mother forgave her— but only after Lucy promised to confin her requests for jewelry to special occasions.

Spelling Words

1. scene
2. bracelet
3. mute
4. strive
5. faithful
6. devote
7. rhyme
8. succeed
9. coax
10. rely
11. conceal
12. forgave
13. lonesome
14. delete
15. confine
16. exceed
17. terrain
18. reproach
19. abuse
20. defeat

1. _____
2. _____
3. _____
4. _____
5. _____

6. _____
7. _____
8. _____
9. _____
10. _____

Declarative and Interrogative Sentences

A **declarative sentence** makes a statement and ends with a period. An **interrogative sentence** asks a question and ends with a question mark.

declarative sentence
The tournament will be held this Saturday.

interrogative sentence
Is your father picking you up after practice?

Thinking Questions
Which sentence makes a statement? Which sentence asks a question?

Activity Add the correct punctuation to the end of each sentence.

1. Mrs. Walker is my favorite gym coach _____

2. I wish we could go to practice today, but it's too cold _____

3. Did you see Mamie or Stephanie at the stadium _____

4. Would Wednesday be a good day to practice your golf swing _____

5. All games will be held in the large gym unless otherwise noted
   _____

6. Can you take over first base since Caitlin is sick _____

7. When her cousin arrives, they're going to go swimming _____

8. When the whistle blows, I always stop running _____

9. When are you going to the volleyball game with Naima _____

10. Did you notice that they are on the same team _____

Imperative and Exclamatory Sentences

Knots in My Yo-yo
String
Grammar: Kinds of Sentences

An **imperative sentence** gives a command and ends with a period. An **exclamatory sentence** shows excitement or strong feeling and ends with an exclamation point.

imperative sentence
Go downstairs and record the football game on TV.

exclamatory sentence
I can't wait for the kickoff!

Thinking Questions
Which sentence gives a command? Which sentence shows a strong feeling?

Activity Add the correct punctuation to the end of each sentence.

1. Help me look for my missing tennis balls _____

2. How messy my gym bag is _____

3. I can't believe I haven't played softball in a year _____

4. Keep running until you cross the finish line _____

5. These golf clubs are the fanciest I've ever seen _____

6. Find a partner and start warming up _____

7. I'm so excited to watch Kevin pitch in this game _____

8. Instead of watching TV, go for a jog _____

9. The last inning was so exciting _____

10. Model your tennis swing after the coach's example _____

Writing with Interjections

Interjections are words or phrases used to exclaim, protest, or command. Strong interjections end with an exclamation point, like exclamatory sentences. Mild interjections can be contained within a sentence and marked with a comma or set of commas.

strong interjection

<u>Wow</u>! I didn't expect to get a skateboard for my birthday.

mild interjection

<u>Oh no</u>, I missed the first pitch!

Thinking Question
What words or phrases are used to exclaim, protest, or command?

Activity Underline the interjections in the sentences.

1. As Miranda ran to catch the ball, she called "Hey! I'll get it!"
2. Aww! Look at those toddlers playing catch!
3. Yikes, you almost got hit by the golf club.
4. Ugh, that practice was harder than I expected.
5. Oh no! I forgot to invite Lara to the tournament!
6. Well, do you think I could borrow your glove?
7. Ouch! The ball hit me.
8. Ah, now I understand what the scoreboard means.

Name _____ Date _____

Verb Phrases and Easily Confused Verbs

Verb Phrases	
He **was running** toward the end zone.	No one **could have stopped** him from scoring.
Easily Confused Verbs	
I **can** remember the cheers.	You **may** come to the game with us.
We **sit** in the stands.	We **set** our program on the bench.
Will you **teach** me that cheer?	You will **learn** the words quickly.
They did not **let** the other team score.	She must **leave** right after the game.
We **rise** early the morning of the game.	The team will **raise** the championship flag.
Why don't you **lie** down and stretch?	**Lay** down your blanket so we can sit.

1–8. Underline the correct verb in parentheses to complete the sentence. Then write the entire verb phrase on the line.

1. Since you asked, you (can, may) put your gear in my locker. _____

2. We could have (sit, set) aside more time for practice this week. _____

3. The coach is (learning, teaching) me to follow through when I pass the ball. _____

4. The visiting team (can, may) defeat us only if we decide not to play our best. _____

5. I had (sat, set) down to talk with the coach before the game. _____

6. He should have (risen, raised) his arms to catch the pass. _____

7. We were (leaving, letting) our emotions take over the game. _____

8. The field (lays, lies) at the foot of a hill. _____

Name _____ Date _____

Lesson 2
READER'S NOTEBOOK

Knots in My Yo-yo
String
Grammar: Connect to Writing

Connect to Writing

Paragraph Using Only One Sentence Type	Paragraph Using Varied Sentence Types
I opened the door to my bedroom. I saw my brother on the floor. He had a guilty look on his face. I wondered what he was up to. Then I noticed he was holding my soccer trophy in his hand. I told him to drop it.	When I opened the door to my bedroom, what do you think I saw? My brother was on the floor. He had a guilty look on his face. What was he up to? Then I noticed he was holding my soccer trophy in his hand! "Drop it!" I yelled.

1–3. Rewrite the following declarative sentences as interrogative.

1. I might actually win this race if I practice enough.

_____

2. This is why I started playing baseball.

_____

3. I wondered who Karen would bring to the game.

_____

4–6. Rewrite the following declarative sentences as imperative.

4. I advise you to take out your notebooks and copy the game plan.

_____

5. I ask that you remove your cleats before leaving the field.

_____

6. You should really watch this skateboarding documentary.

_____

7–8. Rewrite the following declarative sentences as exclamatory.

7. This tennis match is so boring.

_____

8. The Monster is the toughest golf course in town.

_____

Focus Trait: Elaboration
Showing Thoughts and Feelings

Sentence with Basic Facts	Sentence Showing Thoughts and Feelings
The next day, my football team was going to play against Morris High for the championship.	My stomach churned every time I thought about the upcoming championship game between Williams High School and Morris High.

Revise each sentence to show the narrator's thoughts and feelings. Include precise words and sensory details.

1. I went up to my seat in the grandstand before the game.

    _____

    _____

    _____

2. I missed the field goal.

    _____

    _____

    _____

3. I threw a game-winning touchdown pass with five seconds in the game.

    _____

    _____

    _____

4. I felt nervous when I went up to pitch.

    _____

    _____

    _____

5. The crowd watched as I stood at the free throw line.

    _____

    _____

    _____

**Reader's Guide**

The Making of a Book

Charting the Process

The process of making a book has progressed greatly since Mesopotamia. However, the concept of putting words on a surface—making a book—is still similar.

Reread page 81. Use the boxes below to create a flow chart showing the publishing process for making a book in Egyptian times.

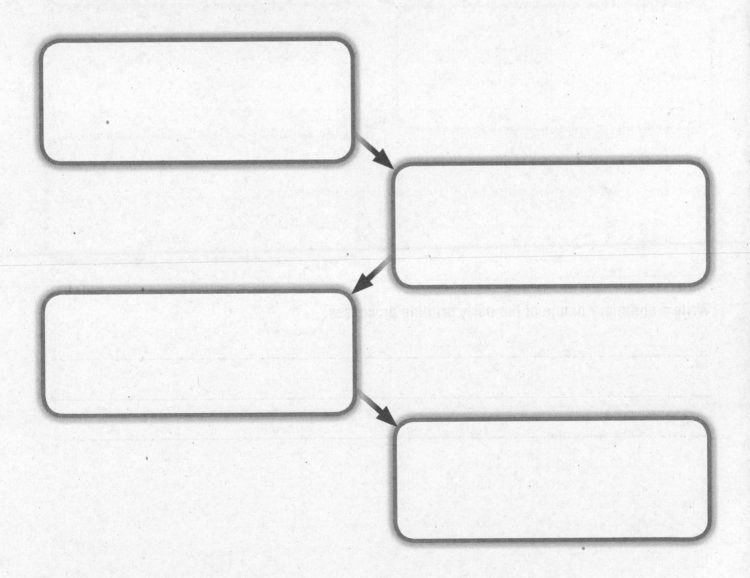

Reread page 82. Create a flow chart for the publishing process for making a book in Europe between 1550 and 1800.

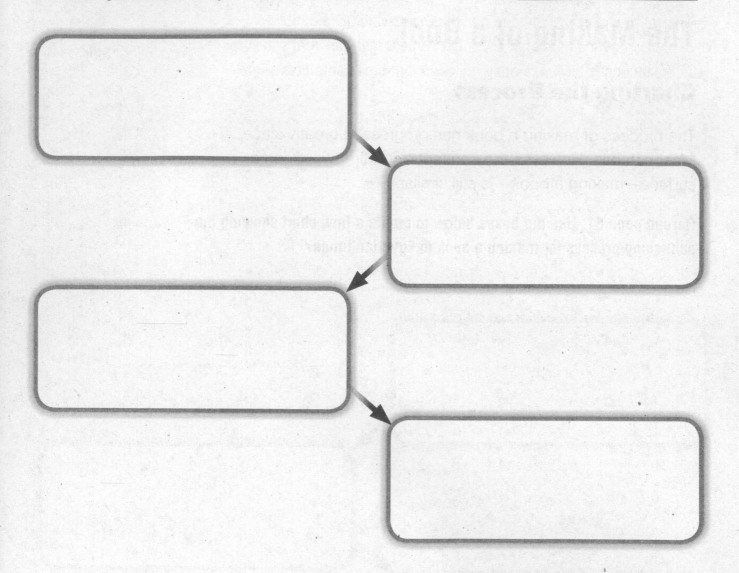

Write a summary of one of the early printing processes.

_____

_____

_____

Multiple-Meaning Words

The words in the box have more than one meaning. Read the sentences below and think about the context and the word's function in the sentence. Then choose the word that best completes each sentence.

report	recall	stamp	strike	minor
camp	bound	patronize	raise	spring

1. Will wrote a _____ about the history of publishing.

2. If he hasn't heard about the surprise party by now, he's _____ to find out eventually.

3. We could not _____ the name of our first-grade teacher.

4. If the government plans to _____ taxes, it must make improvements to the city.

5. The mayor promised to _____ out crime for good.

6. The workers decided to go on _____ until their working conditions improved.

7. We hiked for about five miles through the woods until we arrived at the _____.

8. The boy was too young to make the decision because he was still a _____.

9. In the forest by the waterfall we found a sparkling _____.

10. The millionaire liked to give away money and _____ worthy causes.

The Making of a Book
Spelling: Vowel Sounds /ou/,
/ōō/, /ô/, and /oi/

Vowel Sounds /ou/, /ōō/, /ô/, and /oi/

Basic Write the Basic Word that best fits each clue.

1. using care

2. a shellfish

3. perfect

4. gobble up

5. a dark reddish purple

6. where you might eat in a diner

7. lift something heavy

8. show great joy

9. quiet and serious

10. a type of grass with hollow, woody stems

11. to be unsure of something

1. _____   7. _____

2. _____   8. _____

3. _____   9. _____

4. _____   10. _____

5. _____   11. _____

6. _____

Challenge You are helping a friend run a dog-walking service.
Write sentences that tell about it. Use three of the Challenge Words.
Write on a separate sheet of paper.

Spelling Words

1. mound
2. gloomy
3. caution
4. annoy
5. dawdle
6. counter
7. haughty
8. rejoice
9. devour
10. thoughtful
11. flawless
12. maroon
13. droop
14. doubt
15. bamboo
16. hoist
17. oyster
18. exhausted
19. scoundrel
20. boundary

Challenge

bountiful
aloof
adjoin
taut
turquoise

Spelling Word Sort

Write each Basic Word beside the correct heading.

/ou/ spelled *ou*	
/ō͞o/ spelled *oo*	
/ô/ spelled *au*, *aw*, or *ou*	
/oi/ spelled oi or oy	

Challenge   Add the Challenge Words to your Word Sort.

Connect to Reading   Look through *The Making of a Book*. Find words that have the /ou/, /ō͞o/, /ô/, and /oi/ spelling patterns on this page. Add them to your Word Sort.

Spelling Words

1. mound
2. gloomy
3. caution
4. annoy
5. dawdle
6. counter
7. haughty
8. rejoice
9. devour
10. thoughtful
11. flawless
12. maroon
13. droop
14. doubt
15. bamboo
16. hoist
17. oyster
18. exhausted
19. scoundrel
20. boundary

Challenge
bountiful
aloof
adjoin
taut
turquoise

Proofreading for Spelling

The Making of a Book
Spelling: Vowel Sounds
/ou/, /$\overline{oo}$/, /ô/, /oi/

Read the following story. Find the misspelled words and circle them. Write them correctly on the lines below.

On a glumy afternoon, Cesar began to take his test. He was exhaussted! It had been a hard week of studying the construction of the Native American mownd sites, but he was ready.

Hawty Mrs. Skimple passed out the tests. She reminded the class to use cawtion and not to let their eyes wander over the invisible boundery between desks. Cesar didn't dawdel. As he finished, he knew he had done a flawles job.

He stood up to take his test to the front. The scowndrel sitting in the next seat, just to ahnoy Cesar, stuck out his foot. Cesar stumbled, felt his body droope, and accidentally bumped into the next desk. "I believe you are cheating, young man!" Mrs. Skimple roared. Never before had Cesar felt the pang of someone's dout about his integrity. Luckily, Cesar was able to explain what had happened, and Mrs. Skimple accepted his test.

Spelling Words

1. mound
2. gloomy
3. caution
4. annoy
5. dawdle
6. counter
7. haughty
8. rejoice
9. devour
10. thoughtful
11. flawless
12. maroon
13. droop
14. doubt
15. bamboo
16. hoist
17. oyster
18. exhausted
19. scoundrel
20. boundary

1. _____   7. _____
2. _____   8. _____
3. _____   9. _____
4. _____   10. _____
5. _____   11. _____
6. _____   12. _____

Identifying Simple Subjects and Predicates

The **simple subject** of a sentence is the noun or pronoun that tells whom or what the sentence is about. The **simple predicate** is the verb.

simple subject simple predicate

Most <u>editors</u> nowadays <u>work</u> on a desktop computer.

Thinking Questions
What part of the sentence tells whom or what the sentence is about? What part of the sentence is the verb?

1–4. Decide whether the underlined word in each sentence is the simple subject or simple predicate. Circle the correct answer.

1. <u>We</u> have a library in our neighborhood.

    simple subject   simple predicate

2. My cousins <u>read</u> books all the time.

    simple subject   simple predicate

3. Sometimes my mother <u>sneaks</u> an extra book into my backpack.

    simple subject   simple predicate

4. My <u>dad</u> says that reading is good for you.

    simple subject   simple predicate

5–8. Underline the simple subject of each sentence. Circle the simple predicate.

5. My friend from camp likes books.

6. Fiction is my favorite category of books.

7. In English class, we read many types of literature.

8. The cover of this old book is dusty.

Compound Subjects and Predicates

A **compound subject** contains two or more simple subjects that have the same predicate. They are joined by *and* or *or*.

compound subject

Jared and Toni often work together.

A **compound predicate** contains two or more simple predicates that have the same subject. They are joined together by *and* or *or*.

compound predicate

I read and write every day.

Thinking Questions
Does the subject contain two or more simple subjects that have the same predicate? Does the predicate contain two or more simple predicates that have the same subject?

1–3. Underline the simple subject in each sentence. Then combine the sentences to show a compound subject.

1. Gerard can edit the text. Jennifer can edit the text.

_____

2. Authors work on book manuscripts. Editors work on book manuscripts.

_____

3. Agents negotiate book contracts. Publishers negotiate book contracts.

_____

4–6. Underline the simple predicate in each sentence. Then combine the sentences to show a compound predicate.

4. The author revised the chapters. The author rearranged the chapters.

_____

5. Printers cut a book's pages. Printers bind a book's pages.

_____

6. Editors select manuscripts. Editors improve manuscripts.

_____

Subjects in Imperatives and Interrogatives

An **imperative sentence** gives a command. The subject of an imperative sentence is always *you*, but the subject is never written into the sentence.

Check the mail for manuscripts. (**Subject:** *you* [**understood**])

An **interrogative sentence** asks a question. To find the subject, you must first identify the predicate. Then ask who or what is performing the action described in the predicate.

Where is my book? (**Simple subject:** *book*)

Thinking Questions
Does the sentence give a command? Does the sentence ask a question?

Activity Write the simple subject on the line. Then tell whether each sentence is imperative or interrogative.

1. When is Megan going to call the author? _____

2. Did the designer finish the cover? _____

3. Review this final manuscript. _____

4. Ask her to help market the book. _____

5. How should I arrange these illustrations? _____

6. Does Jorge need more pages? _____

7. Hand me the publishing contract, please. _____

8. Look for more editors. _____

Using Adjectives and Adverbs

good	Ms. Brown is a **good** editor.
	My book sales were **good**, but they could have been better.
well	I think I did **well** on the page layouts.
	I didn't feel **well** after that bad book review.

Articles	Demonstrative Adjectives		Proper Adjectives		
a an	this	that	English	Arabic	North African
the	these	those	Spanish	Persian	Shakespearean

Comparisons					
Adjectives			**Adverbs**		
good	better	best	well	better	best
bad	worse	worst	badly	more badly	most badly
unusual	more unusual	most unusual	unusually	more unusually	most unusually
quick	quicker	quickest	quickly	more quickly	most quickly

**1–4.   Underline the mistakes with adjectives and adverbs.
Rewrite the sentence correctly on the line.**

1. Ms. Diaz is the most nicest Spanish editor in our company.

_____

2. Annette said that I am a gooder editor than she is, but these is not true.

_____

_____

3. I feel well about my writing since my books sell very good.

_____

_____

4. The book about south america was the more difficult one we've published.

_____

_____

Connect to Writing

Sentences with Similar Subjects but Different Predicates	I could edit a book. I could write an article.
Combined	I could edit a book or write an article.
Sentences with Similar Predicates but Different Subjects	Jamal designs book covers. Kathryn designs book covers.
Combined	Jamal and Kathryn design book covers.

Combine the sentences below using conjunctions and punctuation to form compound subjects or predicates.

1. Alison could review the edits. Alison could start a new manuscript.

_____

_____

2. Jamie writes slowly. Jamie edits quickly.

_____

_____

3. I thought we were working on a nonfiction book this week. Todd thought we were working on a nonfiction book this week.

_____

_____

4. Finn loves old books. Jeanette loves old books. Mario loves old books.

_____

_____

5. Egyptian writing is fascinating. Egyptian papyrus rolls are fascinating, too.

_____

_____

35

Focus Trait: Elaboration
Using Precise Words and Sensory Details

The Making of a Book
Writing: Narrative Writing

Sentence	With Precise Words and Sensory Details
The students talked about their story ideas.	The young writers buzzed with excitement as they shared their story ideas.

A. Revise each sentence. Use precise words and one or more words that appeal to the sense named in parentheses.

Sentence	With Precise Words and Sensory Details
1. The author felt hungry when she entered the bakery. (smell)	_____ _____
2. I like the narrator's voice on this audio book. (sound)	_____ _____
3. Kris had a snack as she read her eBook. (taste)	_____ _____
4. I looked at the pages in my new book about sunken treasures. (touch)	_____ _____
5. The artist drew shapes for her book illustrations. (sight)	_____ _____

B. Pair/Share Work with a partner to identify all of the sensory words in the sentence. Identify the sense to which each sensory word appeals.

Sentence	Sensory Word and Sense
6. The girls carefully turned the faded pages of the crumbling book in the musty bookstore.	_____ _____ _____

The ACES Phone from *Noisy Outlaws, Unfriendly Blobs, and Some Other Things ...*

ACES Incident Report

It is Mrs. DeSalvio's and Martin's job to listen for pleas of help from the dogs in their area. Sometimes they can help a dog, but sometimes they cannot. Use details from the text to complete the incident reports for the calls they received.

Reread pages 108–109. Then complete this report.

Incident Report #0101
Name: Martin

Time/Place of call: _____

_____

Description of call: _____

_____

Emotions felt during call: _____

_____

Action followed, if any: _____

_____

Reread page 110 and complete this report.

Incident Report #0102
Name: Martin

Time/Place of call: _____

_____

Description of call: _____

Emotions felt during call: _____

_____

Action followed, if any: _____

Reread pages 113–118. Continue to use details from the text to complete the incident report for the calls Martin and Mrs. DeSalvio received. Include the resolution.

Incident Report #0102
Name: Martin & Mrs. DeSalvio

Time/Place of call: _____

Description of call: _____

Emotions felt during call: _____

Action followed, if any: _____

_____

Resolution: _____

_____

The ACES Phone
Vocabulary Strategies:
Prefixes *de-, trans-*

Prefixes *de-, trans-*

The words in the box begin with the prefixes *de-*, meaning "remove" or "undo," or *trans-*, meaning "across." Choose which word best completes each sentence.

> transmissions   transform   transplant   transcript
> decrease   defrost   demote   decaffeinate

1. The radio could no longer send _____ to headquarters.

2. Coffee brewers soak the beans in liquid in order to _____ them.

3. You need to take care of a garden and _____ the amount of weeds.

4. An official _____ of their conversation is kept on file.

5. The man worked hard at his job. He did not want his boss to _____ him.

6. In May, it is warm enough to _____ the tomatoes outside.

7. Good posture can _____ a person's bad attitude into a good one.

8. It is important to safely _____ frozen meats so they do not make you ill.

Vowel + /r/ Sounds

Basic Write the Basic Word that best replaces the underlined word or words.

I live in a(n) (**1**) <u>city</u> area, so I didn't think I would like camping. The place we were going felt like a (**2**) <u>remote area where no one lives</u>. Local rangers were a (**3**) <u>point</u> of information for us. On our first night camping, the rangers told us the (**4**) <u>device that reflects radio waves</u> showed a big storm coming. The air was cold, and there was a (**5**) <u>very strong</u> wind. I put on my (**6**) <u>hooded jacket</u>. I began to (**7**) <u>long</u> for my warm bed. I declared to my dad I'd never go camping again! But the next morning everything was different. The ground was covered with snow, and there was a thin layer of ice on the (**8**) <u>top part</u> of the river.

"Let's go for a hike," I said, while walking (**9**) <u>straight ahead</u>. "So it seems that you like camping after all!" he said with a (**10**) <u>smug smile</u>.

1. _____ 6. _____
2. _____ 7. _____
3. _____ 8. _____
4. _____ 9. _____
5. _____ 10. _____

Challenge Imagine you have just seen a movie with kings, knights, and dragons. Write a review of the movie. Use three of the Challenge Words. Write on a separate sheet of paper.

Spelling Words

1. source
2. flirt
3. hurdle
4. parka
5. frontier
6. forward
7. radar
8. earnest
9. afford
10. urban
11. discard
12. smirk
13. rehearse
14. mourn
15. surface
16. parcel
17. yearn
18. fierce
19. starch
20. formula

Challenge
horizontal
circuit
reimburse
formidable
monarchy

Spelling Word Sort

The ACES Phone
Spelling: Vowel + /r/ Sounds

Write each Basic Word beside the correct heading.

/ûr/ spelled *ur*, *ir*, or *ear*	
/ôr/ spelled *our* or *or*	
/är/ spelled *ar*	
/îr/ spelled *ier*	

Challenge   Add the Challenge Words to your Word Sort.

Connect to Reading   Look through *The ACES Phone*. Find words with the /ûr/, /ôr/, /är/, /îr/ spelling patterns on this page. Add them to your Word Sort.

Spelling Words

1. source
2. flirt
3. hurdle
4. parka
5. frontier
6. forward
7. radar
8. earnest
9. afford
10. urban
11. discard
12. smirk
13. rehearse
14. mourn
15. surface
16. parcel
17. yearn
18. fierce
19. starch
20. formula

Challenge

horizontal
circuit
reimburse
formidable
monarchy

Proofreading for Spelling

The ACES Phone
Spelling: Vowel + /r/ Sounds

Find the misspelled words and circle them. Write them correctly on the lines below.

Fran awoke as the starship reached the fronteer of the galaxy and began to descard the fluid in which she had been suspended. Her face was still stiff from the startch in the fluid when her first mate raised his ernest face. They couldn't aforrd to waste time. There was a strict formyula for re-entry. They must not miss the gravity dome on the surfice of the wormhole.

They already crossed the first hurdl—everyone was still alive. Last trip, Fran was forced to morne the loss of a crew member. That time they were lucky to return home. No one had thought to reherse wormhole entry. After that disaster, Fran had vowed never to flurt with disaster again. This time they were prepared. After all, the parsel she carried was too important. She had to deliver it to her home planet.

Spelling Words

1. source
2. flirt
3. hurdle
4. parka
5. frontier
6. forward
7. radar
8. earnest
9. afford
10. urban
11. discard
12. smirk
13. rehearse
14. mourn
15. surface
16. parcel
17. yearn
18. fierce
19. starch
20. formula

1. _____ 7. _____

2. _____ 8. _____

3. _____ 9. _____

4. _____ 10. _____

5. _____ 11. _____

6. _____ 12. _____

Recognizing Nouns

A **common noun** names any person, place, thing, or idea.
A **proper noun** names a particular person, place, thing, or idea and is capitalized.

common   proper
My dog is a Pomeranian.

A **concrete noun** names a thing that can be experienced with one or more of the five senses.
An **abstract noun** names a thing that cannot be experienced with any of the five senses.

abstract   concrete
Janine had a wish to visit the zoo.

A **collective noun** names a group of persons, places, things, or ideas, and is singular in form.

collective noun
The ant colony is blocking the sidewalk.

Thinking Question
What kinds of people, places, things, and ideas are named in the sentence?

Activity Label each underlined noun as *common* or *proper*.

1. Abyssinian cats come from Egypt.

_____

2. My report is about lions in Africa.

_____

Activity Label each underlined noun as *concrete*, *abstract*, or *collective*.

3. The zoologist had an idea about the pack of wolves.

_____

4. The museum staff had a plan about the wildlife exhibit.

_____

Capitalizing Proper Nouns

Proper nouns are specific people, places, and things. They should always be **capitalized**.

Organizations	Red Cross, the Boy Scouts
Historical periods and events	the Great Depression, the Renaissance
Buildings	the Louvre, the Empire State Building
Monuments	the Taj Mahal, the Washington Monument
Nationalities	Greek
Languages	Vietnamese
Relatives	Uncle Jim
Regions	the West

Thinking Question
Does this noun name a particular person, place, or thing?

Activity Underline the words that should be capitalized.

1. The aspca helped the animal shelter in detroit.
2. When aunt fran arrived with her dogs, our thanksgiving reunion began.
3. Have you seen prairie dog colonies in the great plains?
4. Herds of mustangs roamed the old west.
5. My dog herbie comes from a litter of scottish terriers.
6. The butterflies will migrate in march.
7. My brother owns the dog-grooming company suds and fur.
8. There is a famous dog statue called greyfriar's bobby.

Appositives

An **appositive** is a word or group of words that follows a noun and identifies or explains the noun. Appositives are usually set off from the rest of the sentence by commas.

appositive

Shadow, the family cat, jumped up on the sofa.

You can use an appositive to combine two short sentences.

I saw Jim in the park. Jim is our dog trainer.

I saw Jim, our dog trainer, in the park.

> **Thinking Question**
> *Which word or group of words follows a noun and identifies or explains it?*

1–4. **Underline the appositive and circle the noun it explains.**

1. Ted, our parrot, squawked as I opened his cage.

2. Marley, my golden retriever, stuck his head out of the car window.

3. The whale shark, the largest type of shark, can grow up to 40 feet long.

4. Do you want to go to Happy Acres, the horse stable near my house?

5–8. **Combine the sentences by adding an appositive.**

5. I took Scruffy to the vet. Scruffy is my cat.

_____

6. We wanted to go to Pet City. Pet City is our local animal shelter.

_____

7. Do you know about hyenas? Hyenas are Africa's wild dogs.

_____

8. Vets seem to enjoy their jobs. Vets are doctors who take care of animals.

_____

Writing Titles and Quotations

The ACES Phone
Grammar: Spiral Review

Titles of Long Works	Titles of Shorter Works
I read the book <u>Diary of a Runaway Puppy</u>.	The chorus sang "The Whistle."
I have seen <u>Speaking With the Animals</u> twice.	We read the poem "Fuzzy Tail."
We listened to Beethoven's <u>Ninth Symphony</u>.	I am reading the chapter called "Brainwaves."

Direct Quotations	The woman said, "I can't find my dog." "He's the cutest little thing," she added. "He must be scared," she explained, "because he's never been away from the yard." "I must find him!" she exclaimed. "Will you help me?"
Indirect Quotations	The woman said that her dog had squeezed under the fence.

1–5.   Write each title correctly.

1. Animal ESP: A Real Phenomenon? (book) _____

2. Behavior Patterns of Lost Animals (article) _____

3. Dog and Cat Monthly (magazine) _____

4. A Pet's Life (poem) _____

5. Hungry Like a Wolf (short story) _____

6–8.   Rewrite the sentence to correct capitalization and punctuation errors. Write *DQ* if the sentence contains a direct quotation. Write *IQ* if it contains an indirect quotation.

6. She said "That her dog Willy was missing."

_____

7. "do you think," he asked, "That your dog is just hiding from you?"

_____

8. "He does like to hide she said he can hide for hours."

_____

Connect to Writing

Using precise words and appositives makes writing clearer and more interesting.
Bob, my rat snake, sleeps all day.
Her dog, a German Shepherd, waits patiently for her to come home.
Ethologists, biologists who study animal behavior, seek to learn behavior patterns.
Mulberry Grove, a local forest, is a great place to watch birds.

Read the sentences. Look for nouns that could be explained more clearly by adding appositives. Rewrite each sentence with one new appositive.

1. The ducklings swam on Lake Thompson.

_____

_____

2. Sparky entertained everyone after dinner.

_____

_____

3. The bee hive was behind the rhododendron.

_____

_____

4. Happy Tails is a great place to volunteer.

_____

_____

5. Ducklings learn to follow their mother by imprinting.

_____

_____

6. The movie was scary.

_____

_____

The ACES Phone
Writing: Narrative Writing

Focus Trait: Organization
Interesting Conflict

A plot is a series of episodes that has a beginning, a middle, and an end. A strong plot includes an interesting conflict, or problem, that readers are curious to see resolved. A weak plot has an uninteresting conflict or no conflict at all. Types of conflict include person against person, person against nature, person against self, and person against supernatural forces.

Weak Conflict: *A dog lives on its own in an abandoned building.*

Interesting Conflict: *A dog is trapped in an abandoned building that is about to be demolished.*

Read each conflict. Add details to help make the plot more interesting.
Write your revised conflict.

1. **Weak Conflict:** A boy's family would like to move to a new apartment.

   Interesting Conflict: _____

   _____

2. **Weak Conflict:** The safari guide heard a noise.

   Interesting Conflict: _____

   _____

3. **Weak Conflict:** The family awoke to the barking dog.

   Interesting Conflict: _____

   _____

4. **Weak Conflict:** A boy helps his family run a shelter for stray cats and enjoys it.

   Interesting Conflict: _____

   _____

Reader's Guide

The Myers Family

Introducing the Myers!

Imagine that you are hosting a meeting of your book club.
Your special guests are Walter Dean Myers and his son,
Christopher. You will be introducing them. Prepare your
introduction by listing facts about the author and illustrator in the
chart. The following pages will help you focus on facts: 139–140,
142, and 144.

Walter Dean Myers	Christopher Myers
_____	_____
_____	_____
_____	_____
_____	_____
_____	_____
_____	_____
_____	_____
_____	_____

What opinion do you have of Walter Dean Myers and his son
Christopher? How is their work inspiring or important?
What do you think about their work and their relationship?
In your introduction, state an opinion or two that will
excite your audience. Support opinions with facts.

_____
_____
_____
_____
_____
_____
_____
_____
_____
_____
_____
_____
_____

Reference Sources

elastic, *adj.* made of a stretchable fabric
epidemic, *adj.* widespread outbreak of an infectious disease
expedite, *v.* process quickly
frugal, *adj.* avoiding waste
intercept, *v.* to stop or interrupt
majority, *n.* an amount equal to more than half of the total
simultaneously, *adv.* occurring at the same time
unearth, *v.* to make known or public; to bring to light

Look at the meanings and parts of speech in the sample dictionary entries above. Choose a word to complete each sentence.

1. The clocks were set to chime _____ at
   exactly 12:00.

2. He hoped to _____ the secret before he returned
   to Mexico.

3. The _____ band on the pants made them
   comfortable around the waist.

4. The Spanish flu of the early 1900s was an _____
   that killed over 50 million people worldwide.

5. I needed to _____ the ball and block the goal.

6. The _____ of the students voted to extend recess
   by half an hour.

7. I went to the post office and asked if they could _____
   the delivery of the package.

8. He was _____ with his money and saved
   every dime.

Homophones

Basic Write the Basic Word that best completes each analogy.

1. *Hospital* is to *administrator* as *school* is to _____.

2. *Mobile* is to *moving* as *immobile* is to _____.

3. *Brush* is to *paint* as *pencil* is to _____.

4. *Bear* is to *mammal* as _____ is to *shellfish*.

5. *Hero* is to *bravery* as _____ is to *fear*.

6. *Mechanic* is to *cars* as *doctor* is to _____.

7. *Blustery* is to *wintry* as *balmy* is to _____.

8. *Ears* is to *hearing* as *eyes* is to _____.

9. *Screen* is to *e-mail* as _____ is to *letter*.

10. *Bracelet* is to *wrist* as *belt* is to _____.

11. *Up* is to *down* as *wrong* is to _____.

Challenge Imagine you just took a trip through the desert. Write a journal entry telling about your trip. Use three of the Challenge Words. Write on a separate sheet of paper.

Spelling Words

1. waist
2. waste
3. patience
4. patients
5. rite
6. right
7. write
8. muscle
9. mussel
10. principal
11. principle
12. summary
13. summery
14. sight
15. cite
16. site
17. stationary
18. stationery
19. coward
20. cowered

Challenge
barren
baron
burrow
burro
borough

Name _____ Date _____

Spelling Word Sort

Write each Basic Word beside the correct heading.

One syllable	
Two syllables	
Three syllables	
Four syllables	

Challenge   Add the Challenge Words to your Word Sort.

Connect to Reading   Look through "The Myers Family" from *Pass It Down.* Find words that sound alike but have different spellings and meanings. Add them to your Word Sort.

Spelling Words

1. waist
2. waste
3. patience
4. patients
5. rite
6. right
7. write
8. muscle
9. mussel
10. principal
11. principle
12. summary
13. summery
14. sight
15. cite
16. site
17. stationary
18. stationery
19. coward
20. cowered

Challenge
barren
baron
burrow
burro
borough

Proofreading for Spelling

Find the misspelled words and circle them. Write them correctly on the lines below.

As we consider the life of Mr. Sung, the principel of our school for so many years, it is hard to wayst words praising his every decision. A sumary of his great career needs to do more than cight his degrees and awards. You can visit the school sitte for that information. We, the students, want to wryte down some of the things we admire about him.

His pateince was almost superhuman. He never used mucsle to enforce his rules. Mr. Sung oversaw the rit of passage into high school for more than five thousand students at our middle school. He was dedicated to the principal that every student deserved the same chance. When we cowerd in the corners, afraid to learn and to be ourselves, he was there to help us grow. We will be grateful to him forever.

Spelling Words

1. waist
2. waste
3. patience
4. patients
5. rite
6. right
7. write
8. muscle
9. mussel
10. principal
11. principle
12. summary
13. summery
14. sight
15. cite
16. site
17. stationary
18. stationery
19. coward
20. cowered

1. _____
2. _____
3. _____
4. _____
5. _____
6. _____
7. _____
8. _____
9. _____
10. _____
11. _____

Singular and Plural Nouns

A **singular noun** names one person, place, thing, or idea. A **plural noun** names more than one person, place, thing, or idea. Most times, a **regular plural noun** can be formed by adding -s to the end of a singular noun. However, if a singular noun ends with an s, ss, x, ch, or sh, add -es to the end of the word to form a plural. If a singular noun ends with a consonant + y, change the y to an i and add -es to form a plural. If a singular noun ends with a vowel + y, just add -s.

Thinking Question
Does this noun name more than one person, place, thing, or idea?

Singular	Plural
She sang a <u>song</u>.	How many <u>songs</u> did you sing?
I saw a <u>box</u> on the stage.	We need three <u>boxes</u>.
Greta's <u>story</u> was about the beach.	Greta's <u>stories</u> are usually about the beach.
My father wrote a <u>play</u>.	My father wrote three <u>plays</u>.

An **irregular plural noun** does not follow the usual rules for pluralization of a noun. Some examples are *feet, children, people,* and *mice.*

Activity Write the plural form of the noun in parentheses.

1. In the play, children got to ride (pony). _____

2. Julie went to three (opera) this summer. _____

3. The painting includes (daisy). _____

4. I am taking two dance (class) this summer. _____

5. How many (person) are in your band? _____

6. Barbara has flute lessons on (Saturday). _____

7. The orchestra judges handed out the (trophy) to the winners. _____

8. Grandpa has a collection of (oboe). _____

Possessive Nouns

A **possessive noun** shows who or what owns or has something. The possessive of a singular noun is formed by adding -'s. The possessive of a plural noun is formed by adding -s'. The possessive of a plural noun that does not end in s, such as *men,* is formed by adding -'s.

singular possessive noun

That is my <u>mother's</u> flute.

plural possessive noun

Our <u>friends'</u> classes are on the other side of the stage.

plural possessive noun that does not end in s

The <u>men's</u> dressing room is downstairs

Thinking Questions
What is added to a singular noun to make it possessive? What is added to a plural noun to make it possessive?

1–4.   Write the possessive form of the noun in parentheses.

1. I wonder how many of these drawings are (Maria). _____

2. The (play) third act lasts one hour. _____

3. Our (class) entry in the art contest came in second. _____

4. Their (families) art collections are worth millions. _____

5–8.   Rewrite each group of words using a possessive noun.

5. the opening act of the ladies _____

6. the drawings of the children _____

7. the gift shop of the museum _____

8. the collar of the costume _____

Common Errors

The most common error when using plural and possessive nouns is incorrect use of the apostrophe.

Incorrect	Correct
My <u>costumes</u> colors are green and white.	My <u>costume's</u> colors are green and white.
Both <u>singers</u> backpacks were filled with sheet music.	Both <u>singers'</u> backpacks were filled with sheet music.
I bought some <u>souvenir's</u> at the museum gift shop.	I bought some <u>souvenirs</u> at the museum gift shop.
Only local <u>hen's</u> eggs are sold at the market.	Only local <u>hens'</u> eggs are sold at the market.

Thinking Questions
What is added to a singular noun to make it possessive? What is added to a plural noun to make it possessive?

Activity **Write the correct form of the underlined noun.**

1. The <u>fans</u> cheers were heard throughout the auditorium. _____

2. We have three practice <u>rooms'</u> in our band hall. _____

3. The <u>orchestras</u> director is a woman. _____

4. Both <u>play's</u> staging was difficult. _____

5. The <u>parent's</u> section of the audience was filled. _____

6. After the concert, the bands went to their <u>bus's</u>. _____

7. My <u>mothers'</u> sculptures are beautiful. _____

8. <u>Toms</u> best paintings are of his family. _____

Using Commas and Colons

Uses for Commas	
Introductory Words	**Yes,** I have read that play by Joe Jones.
Direct Address	**Sam,** give us a summary of the play you read.
Appositives	Harlem, **a section of New York City,** is the setting of this musical.
Series	She gets up early, eats breakfast, and practices until noon.

Uses for Colons	
Hours and Minutes	Our drama class starts at **2:00** P.M., so don't be late.
Introduce a List	For the art assignment, you will need the following: some paper, two sharp pencils, and a good idea.
After Greeting in Business Letter	Dear Mr. Myers:

1–5. Rewrite each sentence. Add commas and colons where needed.

1. No I don't have a theater for my play yet.

_____

_____

2. This year our class has written the following two short stories, five poems, and a play.

_____

_____

3. The play a musical tells the story of a struggling young writer.

_____

_____

4. Our first play rehearsal is from 9 00 A.M. to 1 30 P.M. on Saturday.

_____

_____

5. Costumes props and lights will be planned by students.

_____

_____

Connect to Writing

singular noun	plural noun
My <u>neighborhood</u> has three <u>auditoriums</u>.	

singular possessive
I found the <u>child's</u> drawing under the sofa.

plural possessive
The <u>girls'</u> costumes were packed for them. The <u>children's</u> dog trotted after them.

Rewrite each sentence using the correct form of the underlined words.

1. Our <u>teachers</u> house has a music room in it.

   _____

2. We were invited to one of the cast <u>party</u>.

   _____

3. Last <u>summers</u> musical theater performance was fun.

   _____

4. Some <u>actors</u> costumes were colorful.

   _____

5. <u>Janes'</u> mother sang a beautiful aria.

   _____

6. We played <u>scale's</u> and arpeggios.

   _____

7. Chairs were set up near the <u>stages</u> edge.

   _____

8. The <u>dancers</u> hats were red and black.

   _____

Focus Trait: Elaboration
Creating Vivid Writing

One way to create writing that is interesting and engaging is to provide descriptive details and sensory language to explain story events.

Sentence with Basic Facts	Sentence That Allows the Reader to "See" and "Hear" the Events
The ballet dancer performed a show for the audience.	The ballerina floated gracefully across the stage and then bowed down as the audience gave her thunderous applause.

Revise to create vivid sentences that paint a picture for the reader. Include descriptive and sensory details.

1. Alice put on her make-up for the play.

_____

_____

_____

2. The girl created a picture for her story.

_____

_____

_____

3. The children liked the storyteller.

_____

_____

_____

4. The opera singer sang loudly.

_____

_____

_____

Name _____   Date _____

Lesson 6
READER'S NOTEBOOK

The Boy Who Saved
Baseball
Independent Reading

Reader's Guide

The Boy Who Saved Baseball

Think Like a Reporter

As a reporter, write a script that covers a scene from
pages 168-172. Focus on a specific theme. Use descriptions from
the story to show what viewers would see in the Video column. In
the Audio column, write the reporter's narration. You can also use
quotes from the characters as if they are first-person interviews.

Batting Practice

Video	Audio

Reread pages 176–179 and write the news script.

Lying Under the Stars

Video	Audio
_____	_____
_____	_____
_____	_____
_____	_____
_____	_____
_____	_____
_____	_____
_____	_____
_____	_____
_____	_____
_____	_____
_____	_____

Using Context

**Read each sentence. Use context clues to figure out the
meaning of the underlined word. Then write the meaning
of the word on the lines.**

1. Do you think Mason was trying to <u>deceive</u> me when he gave the
wrong answers to my questions?

_____

_____

2. My mother taught me to be polite and <u>courteous</u> towards my elders.

_____

_____

3. I thought the room in the picture was getting smaller, but it was only
an optical <u>illusion</u>.

_____

_____

4. The rider decided to <u>mount</u> the horse and practice riding once more
before the show.

_____

_____

5. I tried to <u>enlist</u> Sara's help on the project because she is such a good
artist.

_____

_____

Words with *ie* or *ei*

Basic Write the Basic Word that best belongs in each group.

1. recreational, relaxing, _____

2. mislead, betray, _____

3. cover, mask, _____

4. momentary, quick, _____

5. conviction, opinion, _____

6. snatch, clutch, _____

7. arrogant, vain, _____

8. rule, govern, _____

9. observe, notice, _____

10. goods, cargo, _____

11. pasture, meadow, _____

12. despair, sorrow, _____

13. pause, give up, _____

14. distant, far-off, _____

15. fierce, intense, _____

Challenge You have just been to see a famous magician perform.
Write sentences describing the show. Use three Challenge Words.
Write on a separate sheet of paper.

Spelling Words

1. brief
2. field
3. reign
4. review
5. fiery
6. receipt
7. relieve
8. conceited
9. neither
10. foreign
11. grief
12. veil
13. freight
14. belief
15. deceive
16. yield
17. beige
18. perceive
19. seize
20. leisure

Challenge
reprieve
wield
feign
conceive
retrieve

Spelling Word Sort

Write each Basic Word beside the correct heading.

i before *e*	
ei after *c*	
ei spells /ā/	
Other patterns	

Challenge Add the Challenge Words to your Word Sort.

Connect to Reading Look through *The Boy Who Saved Baseball.* Find more words that have the *ie* and *ei* spelling patterns on this page. Add them to your Word Sort.

Spelling Words

1. brief
2. field
3. reign
4. review
5. fiery
6. receipt
7. relieve
8. conceited
9. neither
10. foreign
11. grief
12. veil
13. freight
14. belief
15. deceive
16. yield
17. beige
18. perceive
19. seize
20. leisure

Challenge
reprieve
wield
feign
conceive
retrieve

Proofreading for Spelling

Find the misspelled words and circle them. Write them correctly on the lines below.

Everyone has read a story about a great baseball team, firey competitors who seeze every opportunity on the baseball feild. Defeat is foriegn to them, but they aren't concieted in any way. My team wasn't like that.

I won't decieve you. We were the worst softball team in history. A revew of our record takes no time at all. We lost 48 games. We won zero. We were successful at niether pitching nor hitting. Our uniforms were even baige! Nothing would releive our losing streak. Once, the opposing pitcher pitched a no-hitter! As far as I know, no other team in the history of slow-pitch softball has failed to get a single hit.

Our efforts didn't yeeld a single playoff slot. We finally called it quits after four years. And I had just bought a new glove! I should have saved the receit.

Spelling Words			

Spelling Words

1. brief
2. field
3. reign
4. review
5. fiery
6. receipt
7. relieve
8. conceited
9. neither
10. foreign
11. grief
12. veil
13. freight
14. belief
15. deceive
16. yield
17. beige
18. perceive
19. seize
20. leisure

1. _____   7. _____

2. _____   8. _____

3. _____   9. _____

4. _____   10. _____

5. _____   11. _____

6. _____   12. _____

Action Verbs

An **action verb** is a word that shows action. It says what someone or something does or did. Action verbs tell what event or activity is happening or has already happened.

Char <u>eats</u> hot dogs at the game.

We <u>played</u> baseball at the park on Saturday.

Thinking Question
Which word shows action?

Activity **Underline the action verb in each sentence.**

1. We walked from the auditorium to the baseball field.

2. I predict a win for the Cougars.

3. Gabe threw the opening pitch.

4. Keisha raced across the plate.

5. Rami pitched during the third inning.

6. We all cheer for the players.

7. Jack hits a home run.

8. Both teams played a great game.

Main and Helping Verbs

The **main verb** in a sentence tells what the subject does or is.

You are <u>swinging</u> too soon.

A **helping verb** helps the main verb show an action or make a statement. Some common helping verbs are *am, is, are, was, were, will, should, have, had, has,* and *can.*

You <u>are</u> swinging too soon.

Thinking Question
Which verb tells what the subject is or does, and which verb helps it?

Activity Underline the main verb in each sentence. Circle any helping verbs.

1. The team has played well this season.

2. We have won most of our games.

3. I will leave at the end of the season.

4. I can watch the game at my house.

5. I am attending a game tonight.

6. You should concentrate on the game.

7. You could catch that ball.

8. He should watch the ball.

Being and Linking Verbs

A **linking verb** links the subject of a sentence to a noun or adjective. A linking verb does not show action. It tells what someone or something is, was, or will be.

The coach <u>looks</u> happy today. (*Happy* describes *coach*.)

A **being verb** shows what the subject is or is like. A being verb is a kind of linking verb.

The coach <u>is</u> happy today.

Thinking Question
What word or words link the subject with another word that describes or renames it?

Activity   Underline the being verb or linking verb in each sentence.

1. Baseball is a very popular sport.

2. The pitcher looked quite happy.

3. The hit seemed fair to me.

4. The game became very tense.

5. You appeared calm at the end of the game.

6. Our seats seemed a long way from the field.

7. Baseball can be a very exciting game.

8. I felt good about the game.

9. She is so happy about the win.

10. The team was ecstatic about the playoffs.

Name _____ Date _____

Lesson 6
READER'S NOTEBOOK

The Boy Who Saved
Baseball
Grammar: Spiral Review

Complete Sentences

Complete Subject	Complete Predicate
My brother	plays baseball on the high school team.

Sentence Fragment	Practices every day after school
Complete Sentence	He practices every day after school.

Run-On Sentence	We watched the game last night it was fun to cheer.
Complete Sentences	We watched the game last night. It was fun to cheer.
Run-On Sentence	My brother caught a fly ball he hit a home run.
Complete Sentence	My brother caught a fly ball and hit a home run.

1–4. Label each group of words *sentence fragment* or *complete sentence*.
If the group of words is a complete sentence, draw a line between the
complete subject and the complete predicate.

1. Kids have played at O'Leary Park for years. _____

2. Even my grandpa when he was young! _____

3. The city wants to pave over the field. _____

4. Will make posters to protest and write to our mayor.

   _____

5–6. Correct each run-on sentence by creating a compound subject or
compound predicate. Use the conjunction in parentheses. Write the new
sentence on the line.

5. My family loves baseball my family always roots for our hometown
   team. **(and)**

   _____

6. At the ballpark, my sisters share a bag of peanuts I share a bag of
   peanuts. **(and)**

   _____

Name _____ Date _____

Connect to Writing

Verbs tell what someone or something does. Good writers choose
verbs carefully to help their readers picture the action in their minds.

sentences with vague verbs	sentences with exact verbs
Gracie ran across the field.	Gracie sprinted across the field.
Tyler walked by the bleachers.	Tyler strolled by the bleachers.

**Rewrite each sentence, replacing the underlined verb with a more
exact verb.**

1. Cho looked at the team roster.

   _____

2. She ran across the field.

   _____

3. Danny ran toward third base.

   _____

4. They ate popcorn and peanuts at the game.

   _____

5. Some weeds grew around the outfield.

   _____

6. She drew a picture of the ballpark.

   _____

Focus Trait: Elaboration
Establishing a Claim

> Good writers begin a response paragraph with a claim, or opinion, about a topic. The claim establishes what the writer believes. The rest of the paragraph is organized with relevant reasons and evidence that support the claim.

Read the paragraphs. Rewrite the topic sentence to include a strong claim presented by the writer. Use strong, vivid language.

1. The media is good for people. The reason I believe this is that they bring the important stories that keep us connected to the outside world. For exarnple, I know what's happening in my community, but what's happening a thousand miles away from me? When I turn on the television, I hear the familiar voice of the anchorwoman fill my living room, and I listen intently to the stories. As a result, I feel connected to my country and to the people around the world.

_____

_____

_____

2. Mass media is distracting. When I look all around me, I am bombarded by distracting advertisements. One advertisement promises "Get whiter teeth now!" The next advertisement screams "The most amazing shampoo that you just can't live without!" The products are endless, and it can be overwhelming to decide which one to choose. In the end, I always decide that hitting the great outdoors is the best distraction that works for me!

_____

_____

_____

Lesson 7
READER'S NOTEBOOK

"Do Knot Enter" from
*Math Trek: Adventures
in the MathZone*
Independent Reading

Reader's Guide

"Do Knot Enter" from *Math Trek: Adventures in the MathZone*

Examine the Knots

Sometimes authors use figurative language to help the reader feel certain emotions. Reread page 198 of "Do Knot Enter" and note the figurative language. Identity the feeling it creates.

Figurative Language	What It Really Means	Feeling It Causes
It twists under and over itself again …	_____ _____ _____	_____ _____ _____
Kids are spinning around on a crazy-looking flying saucer …	_____ _____ _____	_____ _____ _____
Hold your horses …	_____ _____ _____	_____ _____ _____
the naughty knotty gate …	_____ _____ _____	_____ _____ _____

Independent Reading
© Houghton Mifflin Harcourt Publishing Company. All rights reserved.

73

"Do Knot Enter" from
*Math Trek: Adventures
in the MathZone*

Grade 6, Unit 2

Lesson 7
READER'S NOTEBOOK

"Do Knot Enter" from
*Math Trek: Adventures
in the MathZone*
Independent Reading

The author created clever section titles using the word *knot*.
Look again at the section titles. Then write the meaning
of each title based on its title and the contents
of the section.

Section Title	Meaning
Do Knot Enter	_____ _____ _____
Knots and Unknots	_____ _____ _____
To Be or Knot to Be	_____ _____ _____
Lord Kelvin's Knots	_____ _____ _____
Knots in Your Body	_____ _____ _____

Word Relationships

Read each pair below. Use the relationship in parentheses to predict the meaning of the boldface word. Write your predicted meaning on the line.

1. fox / **kit** (adult to baby)

Meaning: _____

2. insect / **antennae** (whole to part)

Meaning: _____

3. **racquet** / tennis (equipment to sport)

Meaning: _____

4. plain / **embellished** (antonyms)

Meaning: _____

5. **quill** / pen (item to category)

Meaning: _____

6. **sulfur** / smell (cause to effect)

Meaning: _____

7. stamen / **flower** (part to whole)

Meaning: _____

8. **milliner** / hat shop (person to location)

Meaning: _____

9. **velociraptor** / dinosaur (item to category)

Meaning: _____

10. **sorrow** / tears (cause to effect)

Meaning: _____

Final /ər/

Basic Complete the puzzle by writing the Basic Word for each clue.

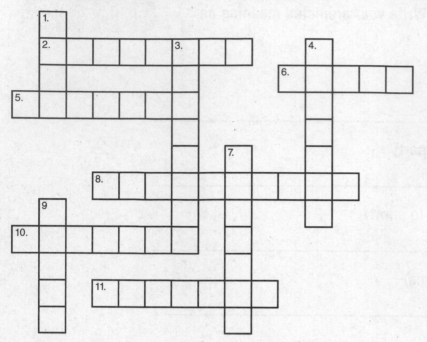

Spelling Words

1. fiber
2. similar
3. regular
4. barrier
5. superior
6. grammar
7. rumor
8. character
9. director
10. acre
11. consider
12. junior
13. senior
14. solar
15. scholar
16. razor
17. surrender
18. particular
19. familiar
20. laser

Challenge
escalator
cursor
geyser
perpendicular
maneuver

Across
2. think about
5. usual
6. used to make cloth
8. specific
10. obstacle
11. the study of forms of words

Down
1. a unit of area
3. a person who is in charge of something
4. alike but not the same
7. a person who has a great deal of knowledge
9. narrow and powerful beam of light

Challenge Write sentences about your class field trip to the science museum. Be sure to describe both indoor and outdoor features. Use at least three Challenge Words. Write on a separate sheet of paper.

Spelling Word Sort

Write each Basic Word beside the correct heading.

Final /ər/ with -er pattern	
Final /ər/ with -or pattern	
Final /ər/ with -ar pattern	
Final /ər/ with other pattern	

Challenge   Add the Challenge Words to your Word Sort.

Connect to Reading   Look through *"Do Knot Enter."* Find words that have the final /ər/ sound patterns shown on this page. Add them to your Word Sort.

Spelling Words

1. fiber
2. similar
3. regular
4. barrier
5. superior
6. grammar
7. rumor
8. character
9. director
10. acre
11. consider
12. junior
13. senior
14. solar
15. scholar
16. razor
17. surrender
18. particular
19. familiar
20. laser

Challenge
escalator
cursor
geyser
perpendicular
maneuver

Proofreading for Spelling

Find the misspelled words and circle them. Write them correctly on the lines below.

After math class, Rich walked to the auditorium. Usually, he would never considar auditioning for a school play, but the directir was his favorite teacher. Plus, Rich was a senyur this year. It would be his last chance. He walked into a crowd of familier faces and took a seat.

"The rumer is that we are doing *The Wizard of Oz* this year," whispered a juniur girl. "I want to play the charactar of Dorothy!"

Rich was quite a scholur when it came to the theater, even though he had never been on stage before. Rich was confident in math, science, and grammer. He didn't feel similer about acting, though. For most of these students, acting was a regulur occurrence. Their auditions would probably be supereor to his.

Finally, Rich took a deep breath and stood up. He walked slowly to the stage and signed up for his first audition.

Spelling Words

1. fiber
2. similar
3. regular
4. barrier
5. superior
6. grammar
7. rumor
8. character
9. director
10. acre
11. consider
12. junior
13. senior
14. solar
15. scholar
16. razor
17. surrender
18. particular
19. familiar
20. laser

1. _____   7. _____

2. _____   8. _____

3. _____   9. _____

4. _____   10. _____

5. _____   11. _____

6. _____   12. _____

Direct Objects and Compound Direct Objects

A **direct object** is a noun or pronoun that receives the action of a verb. To find the direct object in a sentence, say the subject, then say the verb, and then ask *what* or *whom*. Sometimes a sentence may have two direct objects. This is called a **compound direct object**.

direct object

Edward added two <u>items</u> to my list.

compound direct object

Edward divided the <u>drinks</u> and <u>snacks</u> between us.

Thinking Question
What receives the action of the verb?

Activity Underline the direct objects and compound direct objects.

1. Joe measured the distance from his house to mine.

2. I determined the length and width to calculate the area of the box.

3. I measured two cups of sugar for the recipe.

4. Ms. Santos added the vinegar and baking soda to cause a reaction.

5. The new plan increased sales by twenty percent.

6. Richie subtracted the tax from our total.

7. Reese added three more employees to the staff.

8. Sheila ate three cupcakes, leaving only nine for the rest of us.

Indirect Objects

A **direct object** is a noun or pronoun that receives the action of a verb. An **indirect object** is a noun or pronoun that tells to whom or for whom the action is done. An indirect object usually comes right before a direct object in a sentence. To find the indirect object, say the subject, say the verb, then ask *to whom* or *for whom*.

Liz brought <u>me</u> dozens of flowers.

Thinking Question
To whom or for whom is the action done?

Activity   Underline the indirect objects.

1. The teacher gave us ten more math problems.

2. My mother gave me half a dozen chores to finish.

3. Will showed Monica her test score.

4. They asked Mr. Wilson the hardest question.

5. I found Rafael five scarves to add to the costume closet.

6. He bought us four additional tickets for the show.

7. Dion paid me ten dollars.

8. They gave us 100 percent of the proceeds.

Transitive and Intransitive Verbs

A **transitive verb** is a verb that is followed by a direct object.

An **intransitive verb** cannot be followed by a direct object. Intransitive verbs would not make sense with a direct object.

Some verbs have both transitive and intransitive forms, but their meanings are different.

transitive
She <u>runs</u> six (companies)

intransitive
She <u>runs</u> through the park each day.

Thinking Question
Is the verb followed by a direct object?

Activity   Tell whether the underlined verb is transitive or intransitive. Write *T* for transitive and *I* for intransitive. If the verb is transitive, circle the direct object.

1. She <u>saw</u> a tutor for algebra classes. _____

2. <u>Use</u> a calculator for those problems. _____

3. I <u>worried</u> about the math test. _____

4. I <u>reviewed</u> two algebra chapters and one geometry lesson. _____

5. I <u>waited</u> patiently for my math test score. _____

6. I <u>became</u> nervous while totaling my purchases. _____

7. After the last lesson, I finally <u>understood</u> fractions. _____

8. I <u>sneezed</u> violently at the smell of the dusty rope. _____

Simple Sentences

Kind of Sentence	End Mark	Example
Declarative	period (.)	I will give you this calculator.
Interrogative	question mark (?)	Are you ready to add it all?
Imperative	period (.)	Please check your totals.
Exclamatory	exclamation mark (!)	You gave 100 percent!

1–6. Add the correct end mark to each sentence. Then write what kind of sentence it is.

1. This is a complicated calculation __ _____

2. Did I double the recipe correctly __ _____

3. Wait until the sixth measure of the song __ _____

4. That equation is impossible to solve __ _____

5. Let's keep measuring the fabric __ _____

6. Did you subtract the extra time from your work log __ _____

7–12. Rewrite the paragraph below, correcting any punctuation errors.

   I really love this recipe? This cake is delicious? Do you know if we have enough eggs. Well, I suppose I could ask my mom! Please measure the flour. Can you pour a cup of milk! I can't find the measuring spoons?

_____

_____

_____

_____

Connect to Writing

Short, Choppy Sentences
She counted the jars. She counted the glasses. She also counted the ceramic bowls.
Combined Sentence
She counted the jars, the glasses, and the ceramic bowls.

Combine these sentences by forming compound direct objects. Write the new sentence on the line.

1. We need to add eggs. We need to add butter. We need to add the sifted flour.

   _____

   _____

2. She measured the hem. She measured the inseam. She measured the length.

   _____

   _____

3. Jonah calculated the area. Jonah calculated the density. Jonah calculated the volume.

   _____

   _____

4. I paid the check. I paid the tip. I paid the parking fee.

   _____

   _____

5. David counted the pencils in the drawer. David counted the pens in the drawer. David counted the paper clips in the drawer.

   _____

   _____

Focus Trait: Organization
Connecting Ideas in a Logical Order

Good writers organize their argument paragraphs by introducing a claim and following it with reasons and evidence that support the claim. They also use specific words, phrases, and clauses to show how the claim, reasons, and evidence are connected.

Read the argument paragraph. Then use the lines below to revise the paragraph. Begin by reorganizing the first three sentences so that the claim is introduced first. Then find places where you can add specific words, phrases, or clauses to connect ideas.

Here is the proof that math riddles make you think.   You can make an ordinary riddle more challenging by adding the element of math.   I know this because I discovered a math riddle that requires a little critical thinking. Four magicians meet at a party. Each magician must shake hands with one another one time. What is the total number of times they will shake hands? You may have figured out the answer right away. Maybe you gathered your friends to act it out. But just figuring out that the answer is six made you think, right? Math challenges people to use critical thinking skills.

_____
_____
_____
_____
_____
_____
_____
_____
_____
_____

 Reader's Guide

Science Friction

Think Like a Scientist

Scientists are trained to think in a certain way. First, they present a hypothesis, which is a statement that tells what they think is true. They gather data, or details, to support the hypothesis. Then, they analyze the data or draw a conclusion in a lab report.

Reread pages 224–226 in the story. Complete a lab report for the hypothesis listed below. Gather and record data using text from the story.

Lab Report # 1

Hypothesis: Amanda is the leader of the group.

Supporting Data:

1.

2.

3.

4.

5.

Conclusion:

Reread pages 230–234. Complete a lab report for the hypothesis listed below. Gather and record data using text from the story.

Lab Report #2

Hypothesis: Amanda felt bad about how she treated Ellen.

Supporting Data:

1.

2.

3.

4.

Conclusion:

Name _____ Date _____

Lesson 8
READER'S NOTEBOOK

Science Friction
Vocabulary Strategies:
Latin Roots and Affixes

Latin Roots and Affixes

Some of the words below are formed using one of the following root words: *aud,* which means "hear or listen," *lumen/ luc/ lum,* which means "light," and *mov/ mot/ mobil,* which means "move." The other words use one of the following prefixes: *ambi-,* meaning "both" or "around," and *sub-,* meaning "under." Choose the word from the box that best completes each sentence.

ambitious	translucent	audible	motivated
auditorium	subterranean	luminous	submarine

1. The principal's announcement was not _____ because the speakers in our classroom are broken.

2. An earthworm is a _____ animal, since it lives underground.

3. I could see right through the _____ screen.

4. The _____ student took several difficult classes.

5. The stars shining brightly in the sky look _____.

6. I got up early on Saturday morning because I was _____ to be the first person in line when the store opened.

7. Under the water, the dolphin swam by the large _____.

8. We will go to the _____ this afternoon to listen to our class president's speech.

Science Friction
Spelling: Final /ən/, /əl/, and /ər/

Final /ən/, /əl/, and /ər/

Basic Write the Basic Word that best belongs in each group.

1. trash, garbage, _____
2. pint, liter, _____
3. fields, trees, _____
4. circle, square, _____
5. leave, give up, _____
6. advice, help, _____
7. incorrect, wrong, _____
8. enemy, competitor, _____
9. flower, seed, _____
10. tuna, bass, _____
11. end, stop, _____
12. reduce, reuse, _____
13. breathe, air, _____
14. car, truck, _____
15. watch, observe, _____

Challenge Imagine you are running a marathon. Write a paragraph telling about the event. Use three of the Challenge Words. Write on a separate sheet of paper.

Spelling Words

1. triangle
2. mental
3. error
4. panel
5. litter
6. pollen
7. gallon
8. cancel
9. abandon
10. rival
11. soldier
12. recycle
13. salmon
14. counsel
15. rural
16. vehicle
17. citizen
18. monitor
19. physical
20. oxygen

Challenge
punctual
endeavor
abdomen
kilometer
dandelion

Spelling Word Sort

Science Friction
Spelling: Final /ən/, /əl/, and /ər/

Write each Basic Word beside the correct heading.

Final /ən/ spelled *en* and *on*	
Final /əl/ spelled *le*, *el*, and *al*	
Final /ər/ spelled *or* and *er*	

Challenge   Add the Challenge Words to your Word Sort.

Connect to Reading   Look through "Science Friction." Find words in this selection that have the final /ən/, /əl/, and /ər/ spelling patterns on this page. Add them to your Word Sort.

Spelling Words

1. triangle
2. mental
3. error
4. panel
5. litter
6. pollen
7. gallon
8. cancel
9. abandon
10. rival
11. soldier
12. recycle
13. salmon
14. counsel
15. rural
16. vehicle
17. citizen
18. monitor
19. physical
20. oxygen

Challenge
punctual
endeavor
abdomen
kilometer
dandelion

Name _____ Date _____

Proofreading for Spelling

Find the misspelled words and circle them. Write them correctly on the lines below.

Concentrating all his mentel powers, the lab student focused on his science experiment. Carefully, Leo brushed cactus pollin onto his left arm. Even though his teacher had tried to consel him to abandun his mad project, he was determined to change his own physicle properties. Next he mixed a galon of his secret growth formula and drank it. He stepped into the pressure chamber and pressed the control button that would deliver the oxigen. He tried to moniter the process for eror but grew dizzy. Still, nothing could make him cansel his dream. No bully would ever make fun of him again. No rivul would win the coveted science fair prize. He stumbled out of the chamber. A giant, poison-spiked, green cactus arm extended where Leo Finkle's left arm had once been.

Spelling Words

1. triangle
2. mental
3. error
4. panel
5. litter
6. pollen
7. gallon
8. cancel
9. abandon
10. rival
11. soldier
12. recycle
13. salmon
14. counsel
15. rural
16. vehicle
17. citizen
18. monitor
19. physical
20. oxygen

1. _____   7. _____

2. _____   8. _____

3. _____   9. _____

4. _____   10. _____

5. _____   11. _____

6. _____

Using *and, but,* and *or*

The **coordinating conjunctions** *and, but,* and *or* join sentence parts. *And* adds information. *Or* shows choice. *But* shows contrast.

We went to the aquarium, <u>and</u> we observed fish.

Mike can study fish, <u>or</u> he can study aquatic plants.

I was tired, <u>but</u> I finished the experiment.

Thinking Questions
Does the word join parts of a sentence? Does it add information, show choice, or show contrast?

Activity   Underline the coordinating conjunction in each sentence.

1. We waited for you, but you were late to science class.

2. Science interests me, and I enjoy it, too.

3. We sat at our desks, and we decided who would be the team leader.

4. I was willing to lead, but the group chose Andre.

5. We could study a family of mice, or we could study plants in a terrarium.

6. We chose to study the plants, and I was happy about the choice.

7. The team recorded our observations daily, but I missed two days of class.

8. Our teacher said I could review the team's data, or I could write a hypothesis about what happened while I was gone.

9. I chose the hypothesis, and I wrote it that night.

10. I hypothesized that the plants had died, but they actually grew well.

Compound Sentences

A **compound sentence** is made up of two simple sentences joined by a comma and a connecting word such as *and, or,* or *but.*

Ellen talked a lot during the experiment, but George was almost silent.

Thinking Question
What are the two simple sentences joined by a connecting word?

Activity   Underline the simple sentences in each compound sentence. Circle the connecting word.

1. Rob took the science test, but he didn't finish it.

2. He was told to retake the test, or he could write a report about the experiment.

3. Our teacher told us we could study invertebrates next, or we could study ecology instead.

4. Most of the class chose to study ecology, but my vote was for invertebrates.

5. Mr. Wallace assigned my team to study plant life around our school, and we went outside to get started.

6. Kesha observed the plants near the track, but Oliver observed the plants further away.

7. Alex and Sondra studied the ladybugs on the flowers in the school garden, and Jordan took a photo for our report.

8. We could turn in a written report, or we could create a poster with our results.

9. My mom got the poster board, and Jordan printed the pictures.

10. We all thought our poster looked great, and our teacher did, too.

Name _____ Date _____

Subject-Verb Agreement in Compound Sentences

Each subject in a compound sentence must agree in number with the verb that follows it.

My <u>brother likes</u> math, but <u>I like</u> science.

Thinking Question
Does each subject in the sentence agree in number with the verb that follows it?

Activity   **Circle the correct form of the verb in the parentheses.**

1. Mr. Wallace (teach, teaches) life science, but they (teach, teaches) earth science.

2. You (is, are) great at physics, and Juan (is, are) great at biology.

3. The science project (take, takes) a lot of time, but I (like, likes) learning about snakes.

4. Jeanine (help, helps) me with math, and I (help, helps) her with science.

5. Five students (wants, want) to do a project on fossils, but Mari (prefer, prefers) a project on plants.

6. Kyle and Hina (is, are) science team captains, and Hina (want, wants) to meet every day.

7. The science fair (is, are) on Friday, and I (am, are) almost ready.

8. I (are, am) proud of my presentation on butterflies, but my results (were, was) not what I expected.

9. Most butterflies (lives, live) only a few weeks, but one generation (lives, live) for months.

10. Experiments (show, shows) how the world works, and that (make, makes) science great.

Subjects and Predicates

Imperative Sentence	(You) Please clean the lab table.
Interrogative Sentence	Will you clean up this fish tank?
Compound Subject	Dirty glassware and scattered goggles clutter the lab.
Compound Predicate	I will fold the lab coats and organize the supply closet.

1–3.   Write *imperative* or *interrogative* for each sentence. Then write the subject of the sentence.

1. Please bring me the test tubes. _____

2. Should we find an aquarium? _____

3. Sweep the lab area first. _____

4–8.   Underline the conjunction in each compound subject or predicate. Then write the simple subjects or simple predicates that are joined by the conjunction.

4. Test tubes and flasks are placed on the shelf.

   _____

5. Would you rather clean the tanks or wash the beakers?

   _____

6. We sweep the lab every week and help Mr. Wallace with other

   chores. _____

7. Biology and chemistry are both taught in this room.

   _____

8. Jackson and Felicia said the science classroom looked much neater.

   _____

Connect to Writing

Rambling, Choppy Sentences
We could do a biology project. Only Ellen knows about biology. George doesn't say much. Benji isn't much help either.
Compound Sentences
We could do a biology project, but only Ellen knows about biology. George doesn't say much, and Benji isn't much help either.

Combine the simple sentences into compound sentences. Write the new sentence on the line.

1. We could study fish. We could grow beans.

   _____

   _____

2. Maybe George wasn't interested in science. It was hard to tell.

   _____

   _____

3. We couldn't work together. Our biology project was behind schedule.

   _____

   _____

4. Our moldy food seemed like a mess. It got us an A!

   _____

   _____

5. Ellen had many interests. She enjoyed biology and music the most.

   _____

   _____

Focus Trait: Evidence
Expressing an Opinion

Good writers develop an argument by providing reasons and evidence to support their claim, or opinion. They organize their ideas in a logical order.

When writing a book review, be sure to include reasons that tell *why* you think as you do. Support your reasons with evidence from the story.

Read the book review. Then answer the questions that follow.

The new book by acclaimed author Spooky van Danz, entitled *A Very Spooky Tale of Mad Science,* is an excellent follow-up to his debut novel, *A Spooky Tale of Mad Science.* The best part of this new book is the kooky character named Dr. Al Chemy and his wacky adventures.

Once again, Dr. Al Chemy wreaks havoc by setting loose oddball monsters created in his secret lab. The plot gets better when Dr. Al Chemy creates the most destructive creature yet! In Chapter 5, a giant apple monster, with an appetite for doctors, causes chaos at a local hospital.

Aside from Chapter 2, which goes on a bit too long describing Dr. Al Chemy's brother Joe, the book is an instant hit. The vivid story events make this book a page-turner. I highly recommend it.

1. What word in the introduction establishes the writer's claim about the

   book? _____

   _____

2. Which sentence shows the writer using textual evidence to back up

   her claim? _____

   _____

3. What reason does the writer give for liking the book? _____

   _____

4. What part of the book does the writer not like? What reason is given?

   _____

Kensuke's Kingdom

Write a Tip Sheet

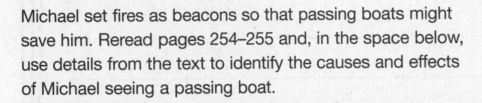

Michael set fires as beacons so that passing boats might save him. Reread pages 254–255 and, in the space below, use details from the text to identify the causes and effects of Michael seeing a passing boat.

Cause	Effect
_____ _____ _____	_____ _____ _____

Michael disobeys the old man and goes swimming in the ocean, only to be stung by a jellyfish. Reread pages 256–257 and, in the space below, use details from the text to identify the causes and effects of Michael getting stung.

Cause	Effect
_____ _____ _____	_____ _____ _____

Michael now understands the dangers of swimming in unknown waters. Use details from the text to help Michael write a tip sheet that describes these dangers.

Question: Why is swimming in unknown waters dangerous?

Answer: _____

_____

_____

_____

Question: What does a jellyfish sting feel like?

Answer: _____

_____

_____

_____

Question: What can be used to treat a jellyfish sting?

Answer: _____

_____

_____

_____

_____

Name _____ Date _____

Lesson 9
READER'S NOTEBOOK

Kensuke's Kingdom
Vocabulary Strategies:
Denotation and Connotation

Denotation and Connotation

A word's denotation is its exact, dictionary definition. A word's connotation is the idea or feeling that is implied or suggested by a word. The words in the box can suggest either a positive or negative feeling, or connotation. Choose the word that best completes each sentence, and then circle whether the word has a positive (+) or negative (−) connotation.

> snicker   furiously   veil   expedition
> isolate   tolerate   grasp

1. The family set out on an _____ to explore their

   new city.   +   −

2. His loud _____ sounded harsh against his sister's

   soft giggle.   +   −

3. If you _____ the meaning of your words, I won't

   understand.   +   −

4. When we ignore another person, we _____ him or

   her.   +   −

5. A firm _____ while shaking hands creates a solid

   impression.   +   −

6. The stormy sea lashed _____ against the shoreline.

         +   −

7. I can just barely _____ the cold temperature.

         +   −

Words with *-ed* or *-ing*

Basic Write the Basic Word that best replaces the underlined word in each sentence.

1. I <u>trembled</u> in the cold.

2. I couldn't believe this was <u>occurring</u>.

3. Jon and I were supposed to go a math <u>teaching</u> session tonight.

4. We had <u>abandoned</u> our plans because of the winter storm.

5. The roads were so bad that travel was <u>restricted</u>.

6. I saw cars <u>sliding</u> on the icy road in front of my house.

7. Dad said it was <u>appropriate</u> that we should have a storm like this on the first day of winter.

8. He said that the snow <u>shining</u> on top of every surface was beautiful.

9. I didn't understand his <u>logic</u>.

10. I have always <u>liked</u> summer over winter.

1. _____   6. _____

2. _____   7. _____

3. _____   8. _____

4. _____   9. _____

5. _____   10. _____

Challenge You have been assigned to report on an awards ceremony. Write a story about what happened. Use three of the Challenge Words. Write on a separate sheet of paper.

Spelling Words

1. happening
2. limited
3. forgetting
4. equaled
5. fitting
6. reasoning
7. labored
8. permitting
9. scrapped
10. tutoring
11. admitted
12. honored
13. skidding
14. pardoned
15. modeling
16. preferred
17. scarred
18. favored
19. glistening
20. shuddered

Challenge
omitted
merited
tapered
equipped
recurring

Spelling Word Sort

Write each Basic Word beside the correct heading.

Final consonant doubled (one-syllable word + -ed or -ing)	
Final consonant doubled (two-syllable word with the accent on the second syllable + -ed or -ing)	
No change to final consonant (two-syllable word with the accent on the first syllable + -ed or -ing)	

Challenge Add the Challenge Words to your Word Sort.

Connect to Reading Look through *Kensuke's Kingdom.* Find words that have the *-ed* or *-ing* spelling patterns on this page. Add them to your Word Sort.

Spelling Words

1. happening
2. limited
3. forgetting
4. equaled
5. fitting
6. reasoning
7. labored
8. permitting
9. scrapped
10. tutoring
11. admitted
12. honored
13. skidding
14. pardoned
15. modeling
16. preferred
17. scarred
18. favored
19. glistening
20. shuddered

Challenge
omitted
merited
tapered
equipped
recurring

Proofreading for Spelling

Kensuke's Kingdom
Spelling: Words with *-ed* or *-ing*

Find the misspelled words and circle them. Write them correctly on the lines below.

The group of young people laborred for hours to climb the scarrd volcanic cliff, wondering what would happen to them. When they had left home, they had felt honorred to be given jobs modelling beachwear in the South Pacific. They admited to one another that it seemed a dream come true to be favorred with the trip, and they pardonned their own giddiness. They thought nothing had equalled the thrill of being chosen, but the boys and girls were forgeting that thrills can also be scary. Then, when the plane plunged into the glisening ocean, they became stranded on an island. They used their best reasonning about what to do. A few of them stayed on the beach to build a small shelter, while some preffered to build a fire on top of the cliffs to signal for help. How long would they be castaways?

Spelling Words

1. happening
2. limited
3. forgetting
4. equaled
5. fitting
6. reasoning
7. labored
8. permitting
9. scrapped
10. tutoring
11. admitted
12. honored
13. skidding
14. pardoned
15. modeling
16. preferred
17. scarred
18. favored
19. glistening
20. shuddered

1. _____   7. _____
2. _____   8. _____
3. _____   9. _____
4. _____   10. _____
5. _____   11. _____
6. _____   12. _____

Phrases and Clauses

A **phrase** is a group of words that does not have both a subject and a predicate. It cannot stand alone as a sentence.

Before lunch, we met our friends at the beach.

A **clause** is a group of words that has both a subject and a predicate.

Before lunch, we met our friends at the beach.

Thinking Questions
Does the group of words have both a subject and a predicate? Can it stand alone as a sentence?

Activity   Tell whether each group of words below is a phrase or a clause.

1. Jon and I were stuck there _____

2. on the beach _____

3. we found shelter under the trees _____

4. after searching _____

5. because of the rain _____

6. with the birds _____

7. because we were thirsty _____

8. we searched for fresh water _____

Dependent and Independent Clauses

A **dependent clause** has a subject and a predicate, but it cannot stand alone as a complete sentence. A **subordinating conjunction** comes at the beginning of a dependent clause. Words like *after, before, because,* and *while* are common subordinating conjunctions.

While we slept, the rain fell hard.

An **independent clause** also has a subject and a predicate, but independent clauses can stand alone as complete sentences.

While we slept, the rain fell hard.

Thinking Questions
Does the clause have a subject and a predicate? Can it stand alone as a complete sentence?

Activity Circle the dependent clauses and underline the independent clauses in the sentences below.

1. While we were hiking, Lyssa and I found some fruit.

2. After we examined them, we put some in our bags.

3. Because we were tired, we stopped near a waterfall to rest.

4. Lyssa ate some fruit while she took a break.

5. Even though we wanted to head back, we decided to hike longer.

6. Before we reached the end of the trail, we heard birds squawking.

7. When we got closer, we saw several parrots.

8. Lyssa took a picture before we ran back.

Complex Sentences

A **complex sentence** contains an independent clause joined by one or more **dependent clauses**. The clauses are joined by a **subordinating conjunction**. These conjunctions tell where, when, why, and how. *After*, *although*, *as*, *because*, *before*, *if*, *since*, *so that*, *until*, *when*, *whether*, and *while* are common subordinating conjunctions.

independent clause   dependent clause

She ate a snack because she was so hungry.

The subordinating conjunction can appear at the beginning or in the middle of a complex sentence. If the conjunction begins the sentence, you should use a comma after the last word in the dependent clause.

Because she was so hungry, she ate a snack.

> **Thinking Questions**
> *Does the sentence contain an independent clause that is joined by one or more dependent clauses? Does a subordinating conjunction join the clauses?*

Activity   Circle the coordinating conjunctions in the complex sentences below. If the sentence is missing a comma, add one.

1. Before we could get on the boat we put on safety vests.
2. Jimi talked to the captain while I fastened my vest.
3. Since we had never seen the whole island we were very excited about the boat tour.
4. Jimi let me use the binoculars so that I could see the fish jumping.
5. If I had ever seen something so awesome I could not remember it.
6. After we had sailed for an hour we were on the other side of the island.
7. The captain docked the boat when we wanted to explore.
8. Until it was time to leave Jimi and I played on the beach.

Common and Proper Nouns

	Common Nouns	Proper Nouns
Concrete	boy, dog, mountain	Michael, Stella, Atlantic Ocean
Abstract	fear, joy, kindness, sleep	Middle Ages, Buddhism
Collective	team, family, flock, bunch	

1–3. Write the nouns in each sentence. Label each noun *concrete*, *abstract*, or *collective*, and *common* or *proper*.

1. Our boat landed on Thunder Island, a deserted island in the South Pacific Ocean.

_____

_____

2. As the captain led our small group up the beach, mystery and intrigue filled my head.

_____

_____

_____

3. The dark jungle stirred my senses, and the suspense was growing.

_____

_____

4–6. Capitalize all proper nouns.

4. A sailor named captain bonnshank told us the legend.

_____

_____

5. His story lasted all the way from pearl cove to the top of mount cyan.

_____

_____

6. My dog skippy heard a rustle in the brush and ran off to investigate.

_____

_____

Connect to Writing

Simple Sentences with Related Ideas
The sky was overcast. We decided to stay out of the water.
Combined Sentences with Subordinating Conjunction
Since the sky was overcast, we decided to stay out of the water.

Combine these sentences by supplying a subordinating conjunction. Write the new sentence on the line.

1. The boat was delayed. We arrived late.

   _____

   _____

2. Dad had a map. I couldn't figure out where we were.

   _____

   _____

3. Pedro asked someone from the boat for help. We were lost.

   _____

   _____

4. Lyssa took some photographs. Grandma sat down on a rock.

   _____

   _____

5. Pedro discovered how to get to the river. We took a new trail to find it.

   _____

   _____

6. It was very hot. Lyssa felt sick.

   _____

   _____

107

Focus Trait: Evidence
Analyzing the Text

It is important to support any claim with reasons and evidence. When stating a claim about something you've read, use evidence from the text to support your reasons.

Claim: *Michael feels angry, sad, and depressed.*

Reason: He wants to get home very badly.

Evidence: *Michael becomes so excited when he sees the ship that he screams and shouts. He is so eager to light the fire that his hand shakes too badly to hold the fireglass.*

Read each question and generate a claim and a reason. Find evidence in
***Kensuke's Kingdom* to support your reason. Write your claim, your reason,**
and at least two pieces of evidence.

1. How do Michael's feelings toward Kensuke change over time?

   Claim:

   _____

   Reason:

   _____

   _____

   Evidence:

   _____

   _____

2. How does Kensuke probably feel before Michael comes to the island?

   Claim:

   _____

   Reason:

   _____

   Evidence:

   _____

   _____

Name _____ Date _____

Lesson 10
READER'S NOTEBOOK

**Children of the
Midnight Sun: Young
Native Voices of Alaska**
Independent Reading

Children of the Midnight Sun: Young Native Voices of Alaska

Design Totem Poles

The author of this text compares and contrasts the lives of two Native American children in Alaska to describe how they celebrate their traditions in a modern context. Use the text and illustrations to help you compare their cultures and lives.

Arts and Culture
Reread page 283 and the first paragraph on page 284.
How do the arts reflect the culture of the Haidas?

_____

_____

Reread pages 290 and 291.
How do the arts reflect the culture of the Tlingit?

_____

_____

Comparison: How are these two tribes similar?

_____

_____

Importance of Family
Reread pages 284 and 259. How is the importance of family similar in the two tribes?

_____

_____

Lesson 10
READER'S NOTEBOOK

**Children of the
Midnight Sun: Young
Native Voices of Alaska**
Independent Reading

Name _____ Date _____

Look at the totem poles on page 282. They are carved from wood and each segment has a special meaning. Design totem poles that explain the tribal lives of Selina's and Josh's families. What could they include? Think about things that make their tribe unique or different. Below each totem pole, write a description of why you chose each symbol.

Selina

Josh

_____   _____

_____   _____

_____   _____

Name _____ Date _____

Lesson 10
READER'S NOTEBOOK

Children of the Midnight Sun
Vocabulary Strategies:
Synonyms

Synonyms

The word pairs listed are synonyms, or words with similar meanings.
Fill in both blanks in the sentences below using the correct word pair
from the box. Then think of another synonym for the word pair. If you
need help, use a thesaurus.

heavy/dense	rare/uncommon	retain/keep	lore/wisdom
often/frequently	decay/rot	abandon/desert	plentiful/abundant

1. The humid air felt _____ with each breath she took. The

   forest was _____ with trees. _____

2. Be sure to _____ your password a

   secret, and _____ the code in memory.

   _____

3. Last year, the crop was _____, but this year, the pests

   are _____. _____

4. They _____ went to the Mexican restaurant, where they

   _____ ordered burritos. _____

5. It was difficult to _____ her home, but the wildfires

   forced her to _____ it. _____

6. We heard many words of _____ when the

   family _____ was repeated on holidays.

   _____

7. It was _____ to make close friends when free time was

   so _____. _____

8. We learned how to brush properly to prevent tooth _____,

   because we don't want our teeth to _____.

   _____

Endings and Suffixes

Basic Write the Basic Word that best replaces the underlined word or words in the paragraph.

My sister's wedding day was finally here. Lots of people thought Stephen and Megan were an (1) improbable couple, but I thought they were (2) charming. I walked into the room and stared in (3) wonder. It was (4) completely full. There were (5) barely enough seats for everyone. Luckily I had a (6) saved seat in the front row. As the bridesmaids walked in, the (7) thrill grew. Then it was my dad and Megan's turn. My dad had a (8) determined air. Megan was so (9) elegant as she (10) moved forward down the aisle. I was very happy for her!

1. _____   6. _____
2. _____   7. _____
3. _____   8. _____
4. _____   9. _____
5. _____   10. _____

Challenge Write a paragraph about one of your heroes. Tell why you consider that person to be a hero. Use three of the Challenge Words. Write on a separate sheet of paper.

Spelling Words

1. reserved
2. unlikely
3. purposeful
4. adorable
5. amazement
6. gentleness
7. sparkling
8. homeless
9. excitement
10. mileage
11. graceful
12. sincerely
13. advanced
14. usable
15. amusement
16. entirely
17. wireless
18. excluding
19. scarcely
20. changeable

Challenge
inspiring
idleness
achievement
precisely
disciplined

Name _____ Date _____

Spelling Word Sort

Write each Basic Word beside the correct heading.

Drop the final *e*	
Keep the final *e*	

Challenge   Add the Challenge Words to your Word Sort.

Connect to Reading   Look through *Children of the Midnight Sun*. Find more words that have the endings and suffixes on this page. Add them to your Word Sort.

Spelling Words

1. reserved
2. unlikely
3. purposeful
4. adorable
5. amazement
6. gentleness
7. sparkling
8. homeless
9. excitement
10. mileage
11. graceful
12. sincerely
13. advanced
14. usable
15. amusement
16. entirely
17. wireless
18. excluding
19. scarcely
20. changeable

Challenge
inspiring
idleness
achievement
precisely
disciplined

Proofreading for Spelling

Find the misspelled words and circle them. Write them correctly on the lines below.

When you look at the adoruble, fur-encased face of the child on the Alaska travel poster, you don't see the whole story. Native American children in Alaska live in an entirerly changebel environment not known for its gentelness. It's a land of vast milage between towns, sparkeling glaciers, and midnight sun. In schoolyards, exclooding wildlife can be a challenge, and a cell phone isn't always useabal because wirless towers aren't everywhere. Although traditional stories show these children carving ice blocks for amusment, there are scarcley any igloos still built in the region. Alaskan Native Americans sincerly want their children to have the same opportunities as children anywhere else.

1. _____
2. _____
3. _____
4. _____
5. _____
6. _____
7. _____
8. _____
9. _____
10. _____
11. _____
12. _____

Spelling Words

1. reserved
2. unlikely
3. purposeful
4. adorable
5. amazement
6. gentleness
7. sparkling
8. homeless
9. excitement
10. mileage
11. graceful
12. sincerely
13. advanced
14. usable
15. amusement
16. entirely
17. wireless
18. excluding
19. scarcely
20. changeable

Name _____ Date _____

Lesson 10
READER'S NOTEBOOK

Children of the
Midnight Sun
Grammar: Longer Sentences

More Compound and Complex Sentences

A **simple sentence** contains a subject and a predicate. It states a complete thought.

Whales are huge. Their blubber is used in many ways.

The **conjunctions** *and, but,* and *or* can be used to make two simple sentences into a compound sentence. **Compound sentences** have two subjects and two predicates.

Fish are plentiful, and they provide much of a Tlingit child's diet.

A **complex sentence** contains an independent clause joined to one or more dependent clauses. The conjunctions *after, although, as, because, before, if, since, so that, until, when,* and *while* can be used to make a simple sentence and a dependent clause into a complex sentence.

Although they dine on fish and other marine animals, the Tlingit people also eat many kinds of berries.

Thinking Questions
Does the sentence have two subjects and two predicates? Does the sentence contain an independent clause? Is the clause joined to one or more dependent clauses?

Activity Label each example a *simple sentence, compound sentence,* or *complex sentence.* If there is a conjunction, circle it.

1. The mountains were covered in snow. _____
2. Seri had seen snow, but he had never seen so much. _____
3. Although he had been to the aquarium before, Seri had never seen sea lions in their natural habitat. _____
4. When he ate herring eggs for the first time, he thought they tasted great. _____
5. Everyone he met was very friendly. _____
6. Seri was feeling adventurous, but he didn't know where to explore.

_____

Compound-Complex Sentences

A **compound-complex sentence** is made up of at least two independent clauses and one or more dependent clauses.

Since it was too cold, we stayed in the lodge, and Jack made soup.

Thinking Question
Is the sentence made up of two independent clauses and one or more dependent clauses?

Activity Label each example a *compound sentence*, *complex sentence*, or *compound-complex sentence*. Underline the independent clauses. Circle the dependent clauses.

1. Before we visited the Tlingit village, Mr. White made us breakfast, and we ate in the lodge. _____

2. After we ate, we dressed in our warmest clothes, and Mr. White led us to the boat. _____

3. Kim was mesmerized by the seals when they swam past her.

   _____

4. Though it was extremely cold, I had a great time, and I would like to go again soon. _____

5. Kim and Jack were ready to go back, but I wanted to stay on the boat. _____

6. Because we were on the boat all day, we were pretty tired.

   _____

7. After we returned, we couldn't stop talking, and Mr. White laughed at our excitement. _____

8. I couldn't wait for the next day's events, and I headed off to bed.

   _____

Name _____ Date _____

Lesson 10
READER'S NOTEBOOK

**Children of the
Midnight Sun**
Grammar: Longer Sentences

Writing Clear Sentences

When writing **complex sentences**, good writers place the most important idea in the **independent clause**.

<u>We won the sledding contest</u> because we practiced.

Good writers also place **dependent clauses** before or after the independent clause, not in the middle.

incorrect: They, after we won, cheered for us.

correct: After we won, they cheered for us.

Thinking Questions
Is the most important idea in the independent clause? Is the dependent clause at the beginning or the end of the sentence?

1–4.   Combine the two sentences to make a complex sentence.

1. I needed help. I had never ridden a sled before.

_____

2. Nic went sledding last year. He taught me.

_____

3. It was very cold. We had to wear many layers.

_____

4. We were sledding. I almost fell off my sled.

_____

5–6.   Rewrite the sentences, placing the dependent clause at the beginning or end of each sentence.

5. Nic, because he sledded last year, did a great job.

_____

6. My sled was, since I hit a tree, broken.

_____

Other Kinds of Nouns

Singular Nouns	alphabet	microscope	bunch	boss	fox	waltz	
Plural Nouns	alphabet**s**	microscope**s**	bunch**es**	boss**es**	fox**es**	waltz**es**	
Singular Nouns	potato	studio	memory	holiday	scarf	mouse	deer
Plural Nouns	potato**es**	studio**s**	memori**es**	holiday**s**	scar**ves**	mice	deer
Singular Possessives	a **baby's** heart		Mr. **Jones's** routine		a **child's** health		
Plural Possessives	two **babies'** cribs		the **Joneses'** plans		the **children's** programs		

1–4. Write the noun in parentheses in its correct plural, singular possessive, or plural possessive form.

1. We climbed on my (parent) boat for a cruise around Prince of Wales Island. _____

2. All of the (child) sat at the front of the boat. _____

3. Several (wave) crashed over the bow. _____

4. We could see some (fish) swimming along the boat.

_____

5–7. Correct the incorrect plurals and possessive nouns in these tongue twisters.

5. **Bobbys** boat boasts the best **float's** from coast to coast.

_____

6. Captain **Steves storys** of the sea seem seriously silly.

_____

7. The **wave's** wispy **whitecap's** whack the **walls'** of **Willys'** whaler.

_____

Name _____ Date _____

Lesson 10
READER'S NOTEBOOK

Children of the
Midnight Sun
Grammar: Connect to Writing

Connect to Writing

Choppy Sentences	Combined Sentences
The mountain was enormous. We could still see its peak. We took pictures.	Though the mountain was enormous, we could still see its peak, and we took pictures.

Combine each group of sentences. Write the new sentence on the line.

1. He comes in from the cold. We should make a fire. We should heat some soup.

   _____

   _____

2. We have dinner. We will play a game. We will go to sleep.

   _____

   _____

3. We can add wood to the fire. You will need to get it. I can't carry it.

   _____

   _____

4. The dogs are hungry. We should feed them. Then we should brush them.

   _____

   _____

5. They have worked all day. The dogs should rest. We should leave them alone.

   _____

   _____

Name _____ Date _____

Lesson 10
READER'S NOTEBOOK

**Children of the
Midnight Sun**
Writing: Argument Writing

Focus Trait: Conventions
Correcting Misplaced Modifiers

Sentence with a Misplaced Modifier	Correct Sentence
Chinese New Year marks the end of winter, which is one of the most important traditional holidays in China.	Chinese New Year, which is one of the most important traditional holidays in China, marks the end of winter.

Read each sentence. Rewrite it to correct the misplaced modifier.

1. Families thoroughly clean their homes to sweep out bad luck and make room for good luck working together.

   _____

   _____

2. Of many colors, the windows and doors have festive decorations.

   _____

   _____

3. Families serve a traditional feast on the eve of Chinese New Year, the most important meal of the year.

   _____

   _____

4. Launched into the sky, the evening is often ended with a celebration of firecrackers.

   _____

   _____

5. Children greet their parents first thing in the morning and receive gifts waking early.

   _____

   _____

Name _____ Date _____

Unit 2
READER'S NOTEBOOK

Freedom Walkers
Segment 1
Independent Reading

Freedom Walkers

Rules of the Bus

Some rules are posted so everybody can see them, such as the *White Only* and *Colored Only* signs on pages 18–19. Other rules are unwritten. Many rules about the buses in Montgomery were unwritten. Reread pages 8–9 to see some examples of the bus rules. Use the information from *Freedom Walkers* to write the rules for riding the bus. Mark each with *W* for *written* or *U* for *unwritten*.

Rules of the Bus

1. _____

   _____

2. _____

   _____

3. _____

   _____

4. _____

   _____

5. _____

   _____

Name _____   Date _____

Unit 2
READER'S NOTEBOOK

Freedom Walkers
Segment 1
Independent Reading

We the WPC Demand!

The Women's Political Council (WPC) made several demands of
the bus company and city commissioners. Read pages 10–13.
Write three demands of the WPC. Use examples of injustice
people had experienced on the buses to explain why the WPC
was making these demands.

The WPC demands an end to unfair bus practices.

_____

_____

_____

_____

_____

_____

_____

_____

_____

_____

_____

_____

Name _____ Date _____

Unit 2
READER'S NOTEBOOK

Freedom Walkers
Segment 1
Independent Reading

Claudette Colvin and Jo Ann Robinson

While many people were affected by the unfair rules on the Montgomery public buses, Russell Freedman describes two women in detail: Jo Ann Robinson (pages 5–8) and Claudette Colvin (pages 15–17). Use the pages to complete the chart, comparing Robinson and Colvin.

Compare Robinson and Colvin	
The lives of the two women	**How They Were the Same** _____ _____
	How They Were Different _____ _____ _____
What they did on the buses	**How They Were the Same** _____ _____
	How They Were Different _____ _____ _____
What happened on the buses as a result of their actions	**How They Were the Same** _____ _____
	How They Were Different _____ _____ _____
What happened after the bus incidents	**How They Were the Same** _____ _____
	How They Were Different _____ _____

Name _____ Date _____

Unit 2
READER'S NOTEBOOK

Freedom Walkers
Segment 1
Independent Reading

Will You Be My Inspiration?

Who is a good candidate to inspire a battle against bus segregation? Read about E. D. Nixon on pages 17–22. Then pretend to be Nixon and analyze each person, listing pros and cons. Use what you have written to describe the perfect candidate.

	Pros	Cons
Jo Ann Robinson		
Claudette Colvin		
Mary Louise Smith		

The best candidate would be:

_____

_____

_____

Name _____ Date _____

Unit 2
READER'S NOTEBOOK

Freedom Walkers
Segment 1
Independent Reading

The Time Machine Reporter

Imagine it is the year 2642 and you are a reporter for the *Time Machine News*. You step inside the machine and travel to Montgomery, Alabama, in the year 1955. You will report on what is happening and post it to the paper's blog.

Use what you have read through page 22 to write notes on what you see and what you experience. What is life like for the people of Montgomery, Alabama in 1955? What important events are happening? Who are important people of the time?

_____

_____

_____

_____

_____

_____

_____

_____

_____

_____

_____

Name _____ Date _____

Unit 2
READER'S NOTEBOOK

Freedom Walkers
Segment 1
Independent Reading

Now use your notes to create your blog post about your experience. Write from the first person point of view. Be sure to use descriptive language to get your readers excited about this time and place.

File   Edit   View   Favorites   Tools   Help

Address e

My Blog

Title: _____

By: _____

_____

_____

_____

_____

_____

_____

_____

_____

_____

June 19, 2642 4:45

Internet

Name _____ Date _____

Unit 2
READER'S NOTEBOOK

Freedom Walkers
Segment 2
Independent Reading

Reader's Guide

Freedom Walkers

Rosa Parks, a Life

Rosa Parks was an important person in the Montgomery
Bus Boycott. Read pages 23–33 to make a timeline
for Rosa Park's life. Use the years on the left side of
the page and write six important events in her life.

Rosa Parks Before the Montgomery Bus Boycott

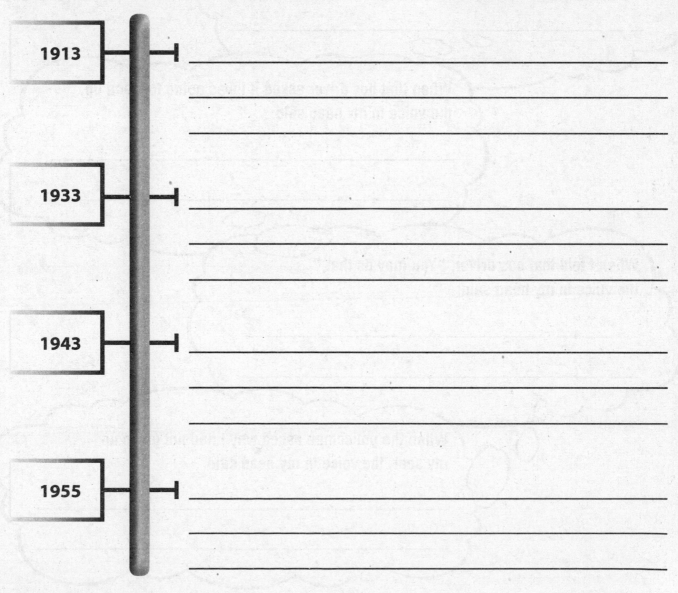

1913 _____

_____

_____

1933 _____

_____

_____

1943 _____

_____

_____

1955 _____

_____

_____

What Was Rosa Parks Thinking?

Read the description on pages 26–28 of what happens on December 1, 1955, when Rosa Parks refuses to give up her seat. You read what Rosa Parks said after she was arrested and what people said during her arrest. Now write an internal dialogue for Rosa Parks.

When that bus driver said, "Let me have those front seats," the voice in my head said:

_____

_____

When that bus driver asked if I was going to stand up, the voice in my head said:

_____

_____

When I told that bus driver, "You may do that," the voice in my head said:

_____

_____

When the policemen asked why I had not given up my seat, the voice in my head said:

_____

_____

Name _____ Date _____

Unit 2
READER'S NOTEBOOK

Freedom Walkers
Segment 2
Independent Reading

You Won't Believe
What Just Happened...

You have read on pages 26–28 how people sitting next to Parks got up and moved to the back. What do you think it might have been like to be a passenger on the bus? Write a letter to a family member about the experience. Tell all the events on the bus, how you felt about it, and include some of your hopes or fears about what might happen next.

_____

_____

_____

_____

_____

_____

_____

_____

_____

_____

_____

Name _____ Date _____

Unit 2
READER'S NOTEBOOK

Freedom Walkers
Segment 2
Independent Reading

Needed: Homemade Posters for Bus Stops

Read pages 36–38 to find out what happened on the first day of the boycott. Find examples of posters people created to inspire each other. Then make your own poster to remind people not to ride the buses. Include graphics and a catchy slogan.

MIA: The Mission

A mission statement explains the purpose of an organization. Read about the beginning of the Montgomery Improvement Association (MIA) on pages 42–44. Write a mission statement for MIA. Name the people involved and why they are organizing. Explain what they hope to accomplish and how they will do it.

Montgomery Improvement Association Mission Statement

_____

_____

_____

_____

_____

_____

_____

_____

_____

_____

_____

_____

Name _____ Date _____

Unit 2
READER'S NOTEBOOK

Freedom Walkers
Segment 2
Independent Reading

Tweets from the Field

You have read about the speech Dr. Martin Luther King, Jr., made
from the pulpit on the evening of December 5. If this speech
happened today, someone would be tweeting about it.
Read what happened during the speech on pages 44–47.
Write short tweets of three events that happened during
the speech. Remember to only use 140 characters
including spaces and punctuation!

Name _____ Date _____

Unit 2
READER'S NOTEBOOK

Freedom Walkers
Segment 3
Independent Reading

Reader's Guide

Freedom Walkers

My Walking Experiences of Freedom

People were asked to testify, or tell about their experiences, at meetings every Monday and Thursday night. Reread pages 49–54 to understand what people said at these meetings. Suppose you were asked to share your experiences of walking. Where are you going every day? How do you get there? Why do you continue to boycott the buses? What do you want others to know?

My Thoughts as a Walker

_____

_____

_____

_____

_____

_____

Name _____ Date _____

Unit 2
READER'S NOTEBOOK

Freedom Walkers
Segment 3
Independent Reading

Dr. King's Journal

Dr. King and the black leaders met with some white officials to end the boycott. Reread pages 54–55 to find out what happened. Then write a journal entry for this day. What would Dr. King write? Compare the meetings with the white officials to the meeting with the black community.

_____

_____

_____

_____

_____

_____

_____

_____

_____

Name _____ Date _____

Unit 2
READER'S NOTEBOOK

Freedom Walkers
Segment 3
Independent Reading

Someone You Should Meet

White people also supported the boycott, such as Virginia Durr and Clifford Durr (pages 25 and 30), Reverend Graetz and Juliette Morgan (page 56), and women who would drive their maids home (page 61). Write an online encyclopedia article about one of these people. Use facts and details from the text to summarize this person's life and his or her importance to the boycott.

Name _____ Date _____

Unit 2
READER'S NOTEBOOK

Freedom Walkers
Segment 3
Independent Reading

Meeting Scheduled for Tonight!

Leaflets were used to tell people about the bus boycott right after Rosa Parks was arrested. Use the leaflet on page 35 as an inspiration. Read pages 62–63. Design a leaflet describing why a meeting has been called. Include the time, place, and discussion topics for the meeting.

Meeting Tonight!

_____

_____

_____

_____

_____

_____

_____

_____

_____

_____

_____

_____

_____

_____

_____

Name _____ Date _____

Unit 2
READER'S NOTEBOOK

Freedom Walkers
Segment 3
Independent Reading

Extra! Extra!

Dr. King learned that his house had been bombed during a meeting. Write a newspaper article about the bombing. Reread pages 64–67 and write a newspaper headline that will entice your readers to read about the bombing. Then write a paragraph that explains the events at the Kings' house.

NEWS

_____

_____

_____

_____

_____

_____

_____

_____

_____

_____

Name _____ Date _____

Unit 2
READER'S NOTEBOOK

Freedom Walkers
Segment 3
Independent Reading

Proud to be Arrested?

The title of Chapter 6 is "Proud to be Arrested."
Why do you think the author uses this title? Reread
pages 61–63 and 67–73. Write a paragraph that
compares the arrests in the two passages. Then explain
what the title of the chapter means.

_____

_____

_____

_____

_____

_____

_____

_____

_____

_____

_____

_____

_____

Name _____ Date _____

Unit 2
READER'S NOTEBOOK

Freedom Walkers
Segment 4
Independent Reading

Freedom Walkers

"The Dumbest Act"

The editor of the Montgomery paper called the indictments, "the dumbest act that has ever been done in Montgomery." Suppose this quote is the subject of a debate. Reread pages 67–73 and pages 75–76. Circle a side of the debate. Defend your side using at least one quote from *Freedom Walkers*.

Arresting protesters is a dumb way to stop the boycott.

or

Arresting many people for protesting is a smart method to stop the boycott.

Name _____ Date _____

Unit 2
READER'S NOTEBOOK

Freedom Walkers
Segment 4
Independent Reading

The News Has Arrived!

News bulletins are short messages about breaking news stories.
Dr. King and his team received a news bulletin during his trial.
What do you think it said? Read pages 72–73 and 83–85, and then
write the news bulletin that was handed to King. Include the
most important information.

Breaking News ... _____

_____

_____

_____

_____

_____

_____

_____

_____

_____

Name _____ Date _____

Unit 2
READER'S NOTEBOOK

Freedom Walkers
Segment 4
Independent Reading

An Interview with the Reverend Robert Graetz

Read pages 83–84 to find out what Reverend Graetz read and how the audience responded. Write interview questions that you would like to ask the Reverend. For more information about his life, read page 56. Then use the information from the text to answer your questions.

Q: _____

A: _____

_____

Q: _____

A: _____

_____

Q: _____

A: _____

_____

Q: _____

A: _____

_____

Name _____ Date _____

Unit 2
READER'S NOTEBOOK

Freedom Walkers
Segment 4
Independent Reading

Nonviolence Workshops

Dr. King spoke about nonviolence, reminding people
throughout the boycott that they should not be the ones
who brought violence to others. Reread page 85. Write
a script that might have been used at a workshop to teach
nonviolence. Remember that a script identifies speakers,
tells them what to say, and includes the actions they perform.

Nonviolence Workshop
Training Script

_____

_____

_____

_____

_____

_____

_____

_____

_____

_____

_____

_____

Name _____ Date _____

Unit 2
READER'S NOTEBOOK

Freedom Walkers
Segment 4
Independent Reading

Life Lessons

Each person in *Freedom Walkers* changed history.
Read pages 96–99. Write the life lessons each of these
people have taught you. Use two examples from the book
to explain your thoughts on each person.

Jo Ann Robinson's Lesson:

Martin Luther King, Jr.'s Lesson:

Name _____ Date _____

Unit 2
READER'S NOTEBOOK

Freedom Walkers
Segment 4
Independent Reading

Claudette Colvin's Lesson:

_____
_____
_____
_____

_____
_____
_____
_____

Rosa Parks's Lesson:

_____
_____
_____
_____

_____
_____
_____
_____

E. D. Nixon's Lesson:

_____
_____
_____
_____

_____
_____
_____
_____

Reader's Guide

The Great Fire

A Timely Fire

This selection starts with the beginning of the Great Fire,
and goes back in time to describe the events leading to it.
As you reread the text, place the events in order on the timeline.

Hints:

Pages 283–288: events of October 8, 1871

Pages 284–288: fires that happened before the Great Fire

Page 290: the aftermath of the fire

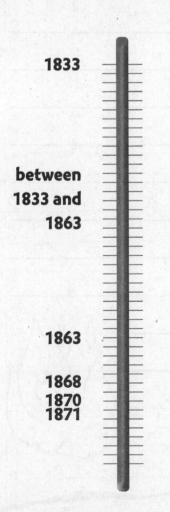

1833

between
1833 and
1863

1863

1868
1870
1871

Do you think the Great Fire could have been prevented?
Write one side of a debate, proving that the fire could have
or could not have been prevented. Use facts from the timeline
and the text to support your claim.

_____

_____

_____

_____

_____

_____

_____

_____

_____

_____

_____

_____

_____

_____

_____

_____

_____

Name _____ Date _____

Lesson 11
READER'S NOTEBOOK

The Great Fire
Vocabulary Strategies:
Suffixes *-ion, -ation , -ism*

Suffixes *-ion, -ation, -ism*

The nouns below all end with the suffix *-ion, -ation, or -ism* which change a verb into a noun. Choose the word from the box that best completes each sentence.

> qualification   heroism   decision   acceleration   stabilization
> criticism   duplication   formation   plagiarism   absorption

1. Being a good swimmer is a _____ required to be a lifeguard.

2. Our teacher reminded us that students who copy someone else's work will be accused of _____ and get a zero for their report grade.

3. The crowd cheered the driver's _____ into first place.

4. Geese fly in a V _____.

5. He made a _____ to turn back when he saw the rising storm.

6. The firefighter showed a great deal of _____ by running into the burning building to save lives.

7. This towel has better _____ than that towel.

8. They planned which presents each member of the family would give to avoid _____.

9. After the earthquake, the tall buildings required _____.

10. She said that she really enjoyed the movie, but she had one minor _____ about the special effects.

Suffixes: *-ion* or *-ation*

Basic Write the Basic Words that best complete each sentence pair.

1–2. I really _____ great actors. Now that I am

going to be in a play, I hope my performance will be

worthy of _____.

3–4. The character I play is a veterinarian who performs

a routine _____. I wanted someone to

_____ my performance to see if I was ready.

5–6. I need to _____ any mistakes before

opening night. I asked Mom to watch me perform my

scene and suggest a _____ I might need to

make.

7–8. Mom said that I did not need to _____

anything about my performance, but that my costume

might need an _____.

9–10. Mom held up a mirror to _____ my image

back at me. I looked at my _____ and saw

that my shirt was on backwards.

11–12. I couldn't find the belt for my costume, so I had to

_____ another belt. I don't think anyone will

notice the _____.

Challenge Your family has put you in charge of planning their next
vacation. Write about where you will go and what you will do. Use
two of the Challenge Words. Write on a separate sheet of paper.

Spelling Words

1. correct
2. correction
3. explore
4. exploration
5. admire
6. admiration
7. subtract
8. subtraction
9. examine
10. examination
11. separate
12. separation
13. alter
14. alteration
15. preserve
16. preservation
17. reflect
18. reflection
19. substitute
20. substitution

Challenge
irritate
irritation
coordinate
coordination

Spelling Word Sort

Write each Basic Word beside the correct heading.

Verb	
Noun (drop the final *e*)	
Noun (no change made)	

Challenge Add the Challenge Words to your Word Sort.

Connect to Reading Look through *The Great Fire.* Find words that have the suffixes *-ion* or *-ation* on this page. Add them to your Word Sort.

Spelling Words

1. correct
2. correction
3. explore
4. exploration
5. admire
6. admiration
7. subtract
8. subtraction
9. examine
10. examination
11. separate
12. separation
13. alter
14. alteration
15. preserve
16. preservation
17. reflect
18. reflection
19. substitute
20. substitution

Challenge
irritate
irritation
coordinate
coordination

Proofreading for Spelling

Find the misspelled words and circle them. Write them correctly on the lines below.

Emma, Rachel, and Granny had gone to eksplore the woods, looking for berries to perserve for the winter. There was no substitoot for wild Maine berries for Granny's cakes. Anything else would subtrack from their unique flavor. Once, she made a substitootion with beets, but it caused the batter to seperate. Now Emma's explurashun had led her astray. She had lost Rachel and Granny. Their separation worried Emma. She paused to refleck and bent to examun her face in a pool of water. That examunation showed Rachel's face just behind her! She was found!

1. _____	7. _____
2. _____	8. _____
3. _____	9. _____
4. _____	10. _____
5. _____	11. _____
6. _____	

Spelling Words

1. correct
2. correction
3. explore
4. exploration
5. admire
6. admiration
7. subtract
8. subtraction
9. examine
10. examination
11. separate
12. separation
13. alter
14. alteration
15. preserve
16. preservation
17. reflect
18. reflection
19. substitute
20. substitution

Name _____ Date _____

Lesson 11
READER'S NOTEBOOK

The Great Fire
Grammar: Subject and
Object Pronouns

Subject and Object Pronouns

A **subject pronoun** takes the place of a noun used as a subject.

subject pronoun

When Maggie saw the fire dog, <u>she</u> patted him.

A **object pronoun** takes the place of a noun used as the object of an action verb. Object pronouns can also follow words such as *at, for, in, to,* and *with*.

object pronoun

When Maggie saw the fire dog, she patted <u>him</u>.

Thinking Questions
Does the pronoun take the place of a noun used as a subject? Does the pronoun take the place of a noun used as an object?

1–4.   Underline the subject pronouns.

1. Maggie tried to put out the fire, but she couldn't.

2. The firefighters were worried, so they kept a careful lookout.

3. Fires are dangerous because they are hard to control.

4. Vera wondered how she could help prevent fires.

5–8.   Underline the object pronouns.

5. The fire is dangerous, so stay far away from it.

6. Maggie got lost, and Cliff helped her.

7. Cliff and I were in trouble, but the firefighters helped us.

8. I told the firefighters that I would write a poem about them.

Pronouns in Compounds

Subject pronouns (*I, he, she, we, they*) should be used in compound subjects. **Object pronouns** (*me, him, her, us, them*) should be used in compound objects. **Antecedents** should be clear to avoid vague pronouns. (*I, me,* and *you* don't need antecedents.)

Thinking Questions
Which pronoun should be used in the compound subject or compound object of a sentence? How can you avoid using a vague pronoun?

subject pronoun

Aunt Sara said that <u>she</u> and Uncle Dan would visit soon.

object pronoun

Aunt Sara told Mom and <u>me</u> that she would visit soon.

antecedent

<u>Aunt Sara</u> told me that *she* would visit soon.

Activity Underline the correct pronoun in parentheses to complete the sentence. Circle any vague pronouns, which don't have clear antecedents.

1. My family lives in the woods. (We, Us) and others must watch out for forest fires.

2. When leaves get dry in the fall, Dad rakes (they, them) and the fallen acorns.

3. Jan and (I, me) help by putting it in the compost to make fertilizer for the garden.

4. Our firewood is far from the house. This keeps both (we, us) and the house safe.

5. Dad says (he, him) and Aunt Sara carried wood a lot farther when they were kids.

6. Having running water is important. (Her, She) and I make sure the hoses work.

7. When the shed caught on fire, Dad told Jan and (I, me) to use the hoses.

8. Sparks were everywhere. We kept (them, they) and the flames from setting it on fire.

9. Nothing was close to the shed, so she and (I, me) did not lose our belongings.

10. If the fire had spread, (we, us) and our neighbors could have lost much more.

Pronouns After Linking Verbs

A subject pronoun is used after a linking verb.

linking verb   subject pronoun
It was he who put out the fire.

A singular noun is replaced by a singular pronoun
(*I, you, he, she, it*). A plural noun is replaced by a plural
pronoun (*you, we, they*).

antecedent   pronoun
The firefighters were they who put out the fire.

Thinking Questions
*Is the pronoun used
after a linking verb?
Does it match the
antecedent in
number?*

**1–4   Underline the correct pronoun in parentheses to complete the
sentence.**

1. The captain of the firehouse is (him, he, them, they).
2. Francis and Bonnie were (they, them, she, her).
3. The rescuer was (they, them, she).
4. The hero of the story is (he, him, we, us).

5–8   Circle the vague pronoun in each sentence.

5. The last one to return was he.
6. Am I next, or are they?
7. She and I need more time.
8. Will they speak first?

Main and Helping Verbs, Linking Verbs

helping verb	I **can** gaze into a bonfire all night long.
main verb	I can **gaze** into a bonfire all night long.

linking verb	I **feel** peaceful watching the flames dance and shimmer.

1–5.   Underline each helping verb once and each main verb twice.

1. My dad and I will check the fire conditions in the morning.
2. Usually we can build a bonfire easily.
3. Would you like to join us?
4. Heather can play many songs on her guitar.
5. We will sing songs all night long.

6–10.   Underline the linking verb in each sentence.

6. Dad looks happy whenever we sit around the fire.
7. His father was a forest fire spotter.
8. Maybe I will become a fire spotter, too.
9. Heather seems to be more interested in music.
10. We look tired but happy at the end of the night.

Connect to Writing

Choppy Sentences	Complex Sentence with Pronoun
Vera saw that my bike had a flat tire. Vera gave me a ride to the fire station.	Since Vera saw that my bike had a flat tire, she gave me a ride to the fire station.

Combine each pair of sentences to form a complex sentence. Add a subordinating conjunction and replace repetitive nouns with pronouns. Avoid vague pronouns by making sure it is clear which noun a pronoun replaces.

1. Maria wanted to learn about fire safety. Maria visited the fire station in her neighborhood.

   _____

   _____

2. Rob's family made a fire safety plan. Rob knew what to do if there was a fire.

   _____

   _____

3. Gina knew better. Gina forgot to replace the battery in the smoke alarm.

   _____

   _____

4. Manny learned how to operate a fire extinguisher. Manny took a fire safety course.

   _____

   _____

5. Never leave burning candles alone. Burning candles left alone can start fires.

   _____

   _____

155

Focus Trait: Organization
Using Standard English

Sentence with Nonstandard English	Sentence with Standard English
I been fixing to learn more about smokejumpers for a good while.	I have been intending to learn more about smokejumpers for quite some time.

A. Read each sentence. Change the underlined word(s) in each sentence to standard English.

Sentence with Nonstandard English	Sentence with Standard English
Smokejumpers are firefighters who parachute into remote areas to duke it out with the fire.	Smokejumpers are firefighters who parachute into remote areas
Smokejumpers do stuff like firefighting, disaster relief, and emergency management.	Smokejumpers firefighting, disaster relief, and emergency management.

B. Pair/Share Rewrite each sentence in standard English. Work with a partner to think of the best words to use.

Sentence with Nonstandard English	Sentence with Standard English
Some smokejumpers are gonna come to our class tomorrow.	
Being a smokejumper must be a cool job!	
Russia has more smokejumpers than all them other countries.	

Airborn

Captain's Log

A plot chart can help you visualize the major events in a story. By creating a plot chart for *Airborn*, you can see the structure of the story. Write a sentence describing each part of the plot.

Climax

Rising Action

Falling Action

Problem

Resolution

Page 346
Problem: _____

_____

Pages 348–349
Rising Action: _____

_____

Pages 350–351, 353
Climax: _____

_____

Pages 354–355
Falling Action: _____

_____

Pages 356, 359
Resolution: _____

_____

The author tells the story from Matt Cruse's point of view. Suppose that, after the rescue, Captain Walken writes about the day's events in his captain's log. As the captain, explain how you feel about Matt Cruse and his actions. Hint: Carefully reread pages 347–349, 353, 356, and 359.

Captain's Log

_____

_____

_____

_____

_____

_____

_____

_____

_____

_____

_____

_____

_____

_____

_____

_____

Prefixes *en-*, *ad-*

Some of the words in the box begin with the prefix *en-*, which means "make," "put in," or "put into." The other words in the box begin with the prefix *ad-*, which means "to" or "toward."

engulf	address	enable	adhesive	enclose
encrust	adopt	endear	adjacent	adhere

1. If you _____ a pet, you must take care of it.

2. Her bad manners did not _____ her to the host.

3. I need something _____ to stick these papers together.

4. The jeweler planned to _____ the crown with precious gems.

5. Next-door neighbors live _____ to each other.

6. Please _____ a check with your application form.

7. Money he made babysitting would _____ him to buy a new bike.

8. Could you please _____ your comments to the audience?

9. It took very little time for the waves to _____ the sand castle.

10. It's important to _____ to your beliefs.

Prefixes: *in-, im-, il-,* or *ir-*

Basic Write the Basic Word that is the antonym of each word or group of words.

1. lawful _____

2. movable _____

3. calm _____

4. confident _____

5. well-mannered _____

6. readable _____

7. loud _____

8. logical _____

9. even _____

10. not appealing _____

11. group _____

Challenge Your class is putting on a mock trial. Write sentences describing the trial. Use three of the Challenge Words. Write on a separate sheet of paper.

Spelling Words

1. illegal
2. indent
3. imperfect
4. irregular
5. inability
6. immobile
7. inaudible
8. impatient
9. individual
10. insecure
11. impolite
12. illegible
13. irresistible
14. impartial
15. illogical
16. inappropriate
17. improper
18. ineffective
19. immovable
20. irrational

Challenge
inadequate
influx
inexcusable
illuminate
irrelevant

Spelling Word Sort

Write each Basic Word beside the correct heading.

in-	
im-	
il-	
ir-	

Challenge Add the Challenge Words to your Word Sort.

Spelling Words

1. illegal
2. indent
3. imperfect
4. irregular
5. inability
6. immobile
7. inaudible
8. impatient
9. individual
10. insecure
11. impolite
12. illegible
13. irresistible
14. impartial
15. illogical
16. inappropriate
17. improper
18. ineffective
19. immovable
20. irrational

Challenge
inadequate
influx
inexcusable
illuminate
irrelevant

Proofreading for Spelling

Airborn
Spelling: Prefixes: *in-, im-, il-, ir-*

Find the misspelled words and circle them. Write them correctly
on the lines below.

Spelling Words

1. illegal
2. indent
3. imperfect
4. irregular
5. inability
6. immobile
7. inaudible
8. impatient
9. individual
10. insecure
11. impolite
12. illegible
13. irresistible
14. impartial
15. illogical
16. inappropriate
17. improper
18. ineffective
19. immovable
20. irrational

"Is this ilegal?" Marco asked in an almost inaudable whisper.
He did not want to do anything immproper. He also didn't want
to be irrashunal or anger the impashent Hortense.

"What a timc to ask!" Hortense groaned. She dangled by
one hand from the ledge of the 100th floor of the building. Marco
was imobile, but Hortense was getting out a glass-cutting device.
She could not be concerned with Marco's ineffactive presence or
his immperfet conscience.

"It might be illogicall, but it would be inapropiate not to try
and save the world if we can. Don't you agree?" Marco knew
that Hortense was right. They had a very important mission. If
the bacteria inside the building were not destroyed, a seemingly
innocent infection could destroy humanity.

"Ugh, this glass is inmovable!" Tired of being imparshul,
Marco bravely helped Hortense finish the task of cutting through
the thick glass. "Nice work, Marco!" Hortense exclaimed. "Now
let's go make this world a better place!"

1. _____   7. _____

2. _____   8. _____

3. _____   9. _____

4. _____   10. _____

5. _____   11. _____

6. _____   12. _____

Name _____ Date _____

Lesson 12
READER'S NOTEBOOK

Airborn
Grammar: Using Pronouns
Correctly

Possessive Pronouns

> A **possessive pronoun** shows ownership. It replaces a possessive noun. Some possessive pronouns are used with nouns, and some stand alone.
>
> **possessive pronoun**
> The crewmen love <u>their</u> jobs.
> This airship is <u>theirs</u>.

Thinking Question
What pronoun replaces a possessive noun and shows ownership?

Activity Underline the possessive pronouns.

1. I told the pilot that I saved his life.

2. Is this your balloon, sir?

3. I knew Matt's father, but Matt has never met mine.

4. The crewmen told me the uniforms were theirs.

5. The doctor told the pilot his injuries would heal.

6. If I can't find a hat, can I borrow yours?

7. Matt held the rope in his hand.

8. The balloon had food and supplies in its gondola.

Pronoun-Antecedent Agreement

An **antecedent** is the word or phrase to which a pronoun refers. A **possessive pronoun** must be in agreement with its antecedent.

antecedent   **possessive pronoun**
Karen bought the book at the airport, so it is hers.

> **Thinking Question**
> *Does the pronoun agree with the antecedent?*

Activity Underline the possessive pronoun and circle the antecedent it refers to.

1. Billy brought his pillow to sleep on the plane.

2. I used your seat belt, thinking it was mine.

3. Franny, is this your first time on a plane?

4. The snack cart lost one of its wheels.

5. Sarah and John practiced their vocabulary on the flight.

6. Karen thought the seat was hers.

7. She and I agreed those seats were ours.

8. I put my glasses in the seat-back pocket.

9. The controls next to you are yours.

10. John wondered if the plane had lost its way.

Pronouns:
Common Errors

One common error is using a pronoun that doesn't agree with its **antecedent** in number, gender, or person.

Incorrect: Da Vinci designed <u>their</u> flying machine long ago.

Correct: Da Vinci designed <u>his</u> flying machine long ago.

Another common error is confusing some **possessive pronouns** with words that sound alike but are spelled differently.

Incorrect: <u>You're</u> muscles aren't strong enough to power wings.

Correct: <u>Your</u> muscles aren't strong enough to power wings.

Thinking Questions
Do the pronoun and antecedent agree in number, gender, and person? Are possessive pronouns spelled correctly?

Activity Find the incorrect word in each sentence or set of sentences. Write the correct pronoun on the line. If the sentence is correct, write *correct*.

1. In 1783, two brothers flew they're balloon 6,000 feet into the air. _____

2. Henri Giffard flew their steam-powered airship in 1852. _____

3. You are from North Carolina? The Wright brothers flew in your state. _____

4. Charles Lindbergh made their first solo flight across the Atlantic in 1923. _____

5. Amelia Earhart made her solo trans-Atlantic flight in 1932. _____

6. Earhart probably crashed when her plane exhausted it's fuel. _____

7. If a person wants to fly, you need to take hours of lessons. _____

8. Is it you're desire to learn to fly an airplane? _____

Verbs and Objects

Direct Object	The crew loaded **supplies** onto the airship.
Indirect Object	The first mate brought the **captain** a cup of coffee.
Transitive Verb	The helmsman **steers** the ship.
Intransitive Verb	The airship **glides** swiftly through the skies.

1–5. **Circle the verb. Label the verb** *transitive* **or** *intransitive*. **Underline direct objects once and indirect objects twice.**

1. The airship's crew started the engines. _____

2. The captain gave the crew specific orders. _____

3. The wind tossed the ship up and down. _____

4. The captain shouted loudly. _____

5. The airship sailed southward. _____

6–8. **Combine each pair of sentences to create a single sentence with a compound direct object. Write the sentence on the line.**

6. An airship's captain needs knowledge of the weather. An airship's captain needs a trustworthy crew.

_____

_____

7. A good crew must have dicipline. A good crew must have focus.

_____

_____

8. For many years, the crew has explored dangerous skies. For many years, the crew has explored exotic lands.

_____

_____

Connect to Writing

Inappropriate shifts in number, gender, and person	Paula wants to learn to fly. To do so, you must take hundreds of hours of lessons. First, students must fly with an instructor. Then we have to put in many solo flight hours before they can apply for a pilot's license.
Pronouns match antecedents	Paula wants to learn to fly. To do so, she must take hundreds of hours of lessons. First, students must fly with an instructor. Then they have to put in many solo flight hours before they can apply for a pilot's license.

Replace pronouns that don't match their antecedents. Write the new sentences on the line, remembering to fix the verbs to match the new pronouns.

1. Paula wants to learn to fly. They visit a nearby airport to learn how you can take lessons.

   _____

   _____

2. The flight instructor introduces himself. They say Paula needs permission from its parents because she is seventeen.

   _____

   _____

3. Paula talks to his parents. We sign a permission form to let Paula take flight lessons.

   _____

   _____

4. James decides I want to take flight lessons, too. Paula goes with him to talk to your parents.

   _____

   _____

Focus Trait: Elaboration
Maintaining a Formal Tone

Informal Text	Text with Formal, Informative Tone
Chuck Yeager was sort of a famous test pilot.	Chuck Yeager is the most famous test pilot of all time.

Read each sentence. Rewrite the sentence to create a formal, informative tone.

1. At some point after high school, Yeager probably enlisted in the Army Air Corps.

   _____

   _____

2. He started up flying in World War II.

   _____

   _____

3. Most people know Yeager because he totally smashed the sound barrier. That means he flew faster than the speed of sound.

   _____

   _____

4. Yeager was in a world of hurt when his engines failed, but he made it.

   _____

   _____

5. Yeager's one of the guys in *The Right Stuff*, a flick about the early test pilots and astronauts.

   _____

   _____

Onward

The Most Important Lists

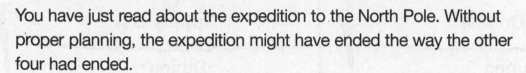

You have just read about the expedition to the North Pole. Without proper planning, the expedition might have ended the way the other four had ended.

Read pages 379–380. Help the teams create a list of at least three tasks to complete before the expedition. For each task, write who will be in charge of completing it. Then write at least three things the teams will need. For each item, write how it will be used.

To–Do List	Supply List
Before	**Before**
_____	_____
_____	_____
_____	_____
_____	_____
_____	_____
_____	_____
_____	_____
_____	_____
_____	_____
_____	_____
	_____
	_____

Read pages 381–384 and 387. Help the teams create a list of at least four tasks to complete <u>during</u> the expedition. For each task, write who will be in charge of completing it. Then write at least four things the teams will need. For each item, write what it will be used for. Use what you have read to help you.

To-Do List

During

_____
_____
_____
_____
_____
_____
_____
_____
_____
_____
_____
_____
_____
_____
_____
_____
_____

Supply List

During

_____
_____
_____
_____
_____
_____
_____
_____
_____
_____
_____
_____
_____
_____
_____
_____
_____

Name _____ Date _____

Lesson 13
READER'S NOTEBOOK

Onward
Vocabulary Strategies:
Figures of Speech

Figures of Speech

Read the sentences below. Think about the meaning of the underlined figure of speech. Then write the meaning on the line.

1. Charlie closed his eyes, took a deep breath, and jumped off the high

   board before he could <u>lose his nerve.</u>

   Meaning: _____

2. Maria's favorite song <u>wrapped its arms around her and rocked her to</u>

   <u>sleep.</u>

   Meaning: _____

3. My grandfather says he doesn't use computers because <u>you can't</u>

   <u>teach an old dog new tricks.</u>

   Meaning: _____

4. Ms. Balin wants us to <u>think outside the box</u> to find creative topics for

   our science projects.

   Meaning: _____

5. Wim should be in the movies—the <u>camera loves him!</u>

   Meaning: _____

More Words with *-ion*

Basic Write the Basic Word that best fits each clue.

1. to crash into each other

2. something that someone owns

3. to cause two people to know each other

4. the distribution of a newspaper

5. to make an approximate calculation

6. to spread around

7. an approximate guess

8. to have or to own

9. the part of a book that comes at the beginning

10. an accident between two cars

1. _____   6. _____

2. Possession   7. _____

3. _____   8. _____

4. _____   9. _____

5. _____   10. _____

Challenge The fire chief has just talked about fire safety and prevention at your school. Write a brief paragraph about what you learned. Use the four Challenge Words. Write on a separate sheet of paper.

Spelling Words

1. circulate
2. circulation
3. conclude
4. conclusion
5. instruct
6. instruction
7. possess
8. possession
9. introduce
10. introduction
11. except
12. exception
13. discuss
14. discussion
15. collide
16. collision
17. oppose
18. opposition
19. estimate
20. estimation

Challenge
detect
detection
procrastinate
procrastination

Spelling Word Sort

Write each Basic Word beside the correct heading.

noun	
verb	

Challenge   Add the Challenge Words to your Word Sort.

Connect to Reading   Look through *Onward: A Photobiography of African-American Polar Explorer Matthew Henson.* Find words with *-ion*. Add them to your Word Sort.

Spelling Words

1. circulate
2. circulation
3. conclude
4. conclusion
5. instruct
6. instruction
7. possess
8. possession
9. introduce
10. introduction
11. except
12. exception
13. discuss
14. discussion
15. collide
16. collision
17. oppose
18. opposition
19. estimate
20. estimation

Challenge
detect
detection
procrastinate
procrastination

Proofreading for Spelling

Find the misspelled words and circle them. Write them correctly on the lines below.

Robert Peary, who led the first expedition to reach the North Pole, is credited with the interduction of local instructors. He was an exseption among explorers because he did not oposse taking help from local people. He was the first to conclud that he could get the best instruktion in Arctic survival from the Inuit who lived there. He took time to diskuss his plans with the Inuit and let them instruck him. He would then lead a discusion with his team and interduce his ideas. He would not tolerate any oposition to his plan. Sometimes there was a colishun of wills, but Peary always won. He relied on Inuit guides and, in the end, excep for one American, most of Peary's companions at the Pole were Inuit.

Spelling Words

1. circulate
2. circulation
3. conclude
4. conclusion
5. instruct
6. instruction
7. possess
8. possession
9. introduce
10. introduction
11. except
12. exception
13. discuss
14. discussion
15. collide
16. collision
17. oppose
18. opposition
19. estimate
20. estimation

1. _____   7. _____
2. _____   8. _____
3. _____   9. _____
4. _____   10. _____
5. _____   11. _____
6. _____   12. _____

Present, Past, and Future Tenses

The **present tense** tells that something is happening now.
The **past tense** tells that something has already happened.
The **future tense** tells that something is going to happen.

past

He <u>asked</u> them to join the expedition a week ago.

present

Today, he <u>asks</u> them if they have finished packing.

future

When they return from the expedition, he <u>will ask</u> them if they enjoyed the trip.

Thinking Question
Does the sentence tell about something that is happening now, something that has already happened, or something that is going to happen?

Activity Write *present, past,* or *future* for each underlined verb.

1. We <u>loaded</u> the sledges. _____Past_____

2. He <u>looks</u> at the map. _____Present_____

3. We <u>will stay</u> in an igloo. _____future_____

4. They never <u>talk</u> about failure. _____

5. We'll <u>explore</u> the caves tomorrow. _____future_____

6. Pressure ridges <u>slow</u> them down. _____Present_____

7. <u>Will</u> we <u>arrive</u> there next week? _____future_____

8. I <u>shall lead</u> the team. _____

9. Henson <u>explored</u> the Arctic. _____

10. They <u>fear</u> crevasses. _____

Perfect Tenses

The **present perfect** describes an action that started in the past and may still be going on. This tense is formed by using *has* or *have* with the past participle of the verb.

We <u>have studied</u> grammar for many weeks.

The **past perfect** describes an action that was completed before some moment or action in the past. This tense is formed by using *had* with the past participle of the verb.

Before that, we <u>had studied</u> vocabulary.

The **future perfect** describes an action that will be completed before some moment or action in the future. This tense is formed by using *will have* with the past participle of the verb.

By next semester, we <u>will have studied</u> a lot of grammar and vocabulary.

Thinking Question
How are the perfect tenses formed?

Activity Write *present perfect*, *past perfect*, or *future perfect* for each underlined verb.

1. Bob <u>had completed</u> the hike in three hours. _____

2. Julie <u>has hiked</u> with our team for months. _____

3. They <u>have traveled</u> very far. _____

4. By April, we <u>will have collected</u> enough money for the trip. _____

5. The students <u>had studied</u> about the North Pole. _____

6. People <u>have said</u> it's a very unique rock formation. _____

7. They <u>will have finished</u> by then. _____

8. By the time we got top of the mountain, the sun <u>had set</u>. _____

Using Consistent Tenses

> **Using consistent tenses** means making sure that all verbs
> are in the same tense: either past, present, or future.
>
> **consistent tense**
> I walked home, made dinner, and finished my homework.

Thinking Question
*How do I make the
tense of the verbs in a
sentence consistent?*

Activity Rewrite the underlined verb to make it consistent with the verb
tense in the sentence.

1. They reached the pole on the fifth day and <u>stay</u> there. ___served___

2. He aims to do it in six months and <u>hoped</u> to do it sooner. _____

3. Henson fixed the broken sled and <u>drags</u> it to the yard. _____

4. We cooked the food on a small stove and <u>serve</u> it. _____

5. He looks at the ridge of ice and <u>wondered</u>. _____

6. The explorers play with the dogs and <u>chased</u> them. _____

7. The dog at the head of the team limps and <u>will struggle</u>. _____

8. The team was exhausted after the hard day and <u>yearn</u> for home. _____

9. Peary showed he was pleased with their efforts when he <u>hugs</u> the dogs.

   _____

10. The dogs were tired and <u>take</u> a nap. _____

Coordinating Conjunctions

Dr. Hollister **and** his team set out on an adventure.
Have the sled dogs eaten, **or** do they need to be fed?
The team wanted to leave immediately, **but** the doctor wanted to wait until morning.

1–4. Circle the coordinating conjunction that has the meaning shown in parentheses. Then write whether the conjunction is used to connect *subjects, predicates,* or *simple sentences.*

1. The tundra is dangerous, but the explorers are a brave group of adventurers. **(shows contrast)** _____

2. This fur coat keeps you warm and shields you from the wind.
   (adds information) _____

3. Will the lead team carry the supplies, or will the support team carry them? **(shows choice)** _____

4. Are the lead team and the support team ready, or should we wait?
   (adds information) _____

5–6. Combine the underlined sentences in the passage to make compound sentences. For each sentence, use a comma and a coordinating conjunction, or use a semicolon.

   The expedition began in the morning. Everybody was anxious about the journey ahead. The sled dogs barked. They trotted through the snow. The sun had not yet risen. The team had headlamps to light their way.

5. _____

   _____

6. _____

   _____

Connect to Writing

Incorrect Tenses	Correct Tenses
"Henson and I <u>walk</u> ahead," said Peary. We all <u>carry</u> our packs onward as heavy clouds <u>will blot</u> out the sun.	"Henson and I <u>will walk</u> ahead," said Peary. We all <u>carried</u> our packs onward as heavy clouds <u>blotted</u> out the sun.

Rewrite each sentence using the correct tense of the verb in parentheses.

1. Henson was wearied by the terrain and (hope) the weather would improve.

_____

_____

2. The team walked ten miles today, and they (walk) twenty miles tomorrow.

_____

_____

3. We (wait) a long time for Peary's team yesterday.

_____

_____

4. The Inuit will leave soon, and we (miss) their valuable help.

_____

_____

5. Did you feed the dogs when they (bark)?

_____

_____

6. They were cold and hungry when they (arrive) at the igloo.

_____

_____

Focus Trait: Organization
Grouping Ideas into Paragraphs

Ideas	Ideas Organized into Logical Order in a Paragraph
• Kit Carson lived from 1809–1868. • Carson was hired to be a guide for John C. Fremont. • Carson became a national hero when Fremont wrote about the trip. • He worked as a fur trapper in New Mexico. • He led Fremont to Oregon, over 1300 miles of mountains and wilderness.	Kit Carson lived from 1809–1868. He worked as a fur trapper in New Mexico. Carson was hired to be a guide for John C. Fremont. He led Fremont to Oregon, over 1300 miles of mountains and wilderness. Carson became a national hero when Fremont wrote about the trip.

Read the following sentences. Then rewrite them as two separate paragraphs. Keep similar ideas grouped together in an order that makes sense.

Ideas	Ideas Organized into Logical Order in Paragraphs
• She flew on the space shuttle Endeavour as the Mission Specialist. • Mae Jemison was born in 1956. • As a girl, she loved to read books about the universe. • Jemison was the first African–American woman in space. • The mission lifted off on September 12, 1992, and landed on September 20, 1992. • She later studied science and medicine.	_____ _____ _____ _____ _____ _____ _____ _____ _____

Pair/Share Work with a partner to write a new sentence that could be added to each paragraph.

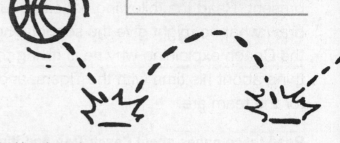

Any Small Goodness

Thanks for the Memories!

It is the end of basketball season. Coach Tree is leaving the school but not before one last party! People at the party will present Coach Tree with a signed book commemorating his year at the school.

Choose two characters from "Any Small Goodness" and read the pages shown. Then write as those characters, telling what they will remember about Coach Tree. Use clues from the story to figure out their thoughts and feelings.

Luis: pages 410–411, 417	Arturo: pages 410–413, 417	Jose: pages 413–414

Alicia: page 414

To the Coach

To the Coach

From:

From:

At the same party, Coach Tree gave the Tigers his own present. Read the following pages about Coach Tree and draw what he might give the school. Then write a letter from the Coach explaining why he is giving this present, his favorite thing about his time with the Tigers, and what his hopes for the team are.

Read these pages about Coach Tree and the Tigers: 409, 412, 415–416.

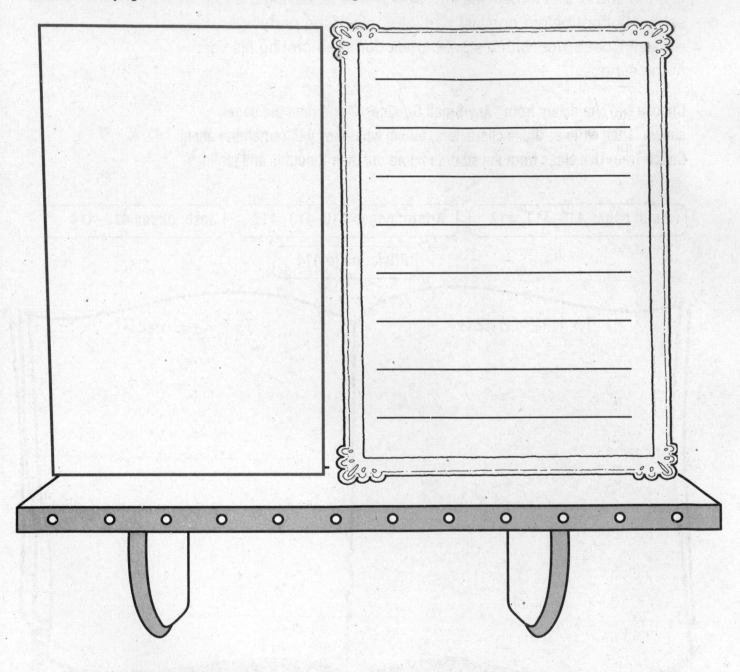

Word Relationships

For the sentences below, fill in both blanks using a word pair from the box that makes the most sense. Then write the kind of word relationship the word pairs share.

bland, spicy	smell, see	banjo, red	utensil, tool
hand, hour	reject, accept	smiling, crying	swim team, band

1. _____ is to a pepper as _____ is to potato. _____

2. Happiness is to _____ as sadness is to _____.
_____

3. Refuse is to _____ as approve is to _____.
_____

4. _____ is to instrument as _____ is to color. _____

5. Finger is to _____ as minute is to _____.
_____

6. Sniff is to _____ as look is to _____.
_____

7. Fork is to _____ as hammer is to _____.
_____

8. Swimmer is to _____ as guitarist is to _____.
_____

Word Parts *com-*, *con-*

Basic Complete the puzzle by writing the Basic Word for each clue.

Spelling Words

1. contrast
2. contact
3. compound
4. concentrate
5. combine
6. comment
7. conference
8. compete
9. community
10. convert
11. conversation
12. commute
13. constitution
14. conduct
15. consumer
16. continent
17. composition
18. communicate
19. compliment
20. condition

Challenge

confidential
commission
compatible
combustion
comprehension

Across

3. situation
6. differ
7. someone who buys goods and services
8. to focus
9. a meeting
10. to convey

Down

1. get in touch with
2. basic laws of government
4. mixture
5. to travel regularly
6. a large land mass

Challenge Imagine you work in a shop that caters to celebrities. Write sentences about clients and store policies. Use three Challenge Words. Write on a separate sheet of paper.

Spelling Word Sort

Write each Basic Word beside the correct heading.

Words with *con-*	
Words with *com-* before *b*	
Words with *com-* before *m*	
Words with *com-* before *p*	

Spelling Words

1. contrast
2. contact
3. compound
4. concentrate
5. combine
6. comment
7. conference
8. compete
9. community
10. convert
11. conversation
12. commute
13. constitution
14. conduct
15. consumer
16. continent
17. composition
18. communicate
19. compliment
20. condition

Challenge
confidential
commission
compatible
combustion
comprehension

Challenge   Add the Challenge Words to your Word Sort.

Connect to Reading   Look through *Any Small Goodness.* Find words that have the *com-* or *con-* word parts. Add them to your Word Sort.

Proofreading for Spelling

Find the misspelled words and circle them. Write them correctly on the lines below.

Hector decided he wouldn't make a coment about how Los Angeles and Chicago conntrast. Of course, Papa couldn't comute across the contenent to his new job. Hector's desire to stay with his friends couldn't compect with the needs of his family. So here they were in LA. The compossition of the new comunity was different from the neighborhood in Chicago. In convirsation here, people would commbine English and Spanish to comunicate in ways Hector didn't understand. His new school didn't have a strong music program, and his dream was to condukt a symphony someday. Yet when his family went to a concert in the local park, many people were there. Hector saw a sign for music lessons that included contakt information. He smiled when he saw that the address for the lessons was in his neighborhood. It was Hector's first moment of hope in Los Angeles.

Spelling Words

1. contrast
2. contact
3. compound
4. concentrate
5. combine
6. comment
7. conference
8. compete
9. community
10. convert
11. conversation
12. commute
13. constitution
14. conduct
15. consumer
16. continent
17. composition
18. communicate
19. compliment
20. condition

1. _____   7. _____
2. _____   8. _____
3. _____   9. _____
4. _____   10. _____
5. _____   11. _____
6. _____   12. _____

Name _____ Date _____

Lesson 14
READER'S NOTEBOOK

Any Small Goodness
Grammar: Subject-Verb
Agreement

Active/Passive Voice

Active verbs describe an action that a subject does directly. **Passive verbs** describe an action that is being done to, or happened to, the subject.

active voice
I <u>threw</u> the ball.

passive voice
The ball <u>was thrown</u> by me.

Thinking Question
Does this verb describe an action the subject does or an action being done to the subject?

Activity Rewrite the sentences to be in the active voice instead of passive.

1. Tom was hit by the basketball. _____

2. They were surprised by the score. _____

3. The game was won by the Ravens. _____

4. The ball was dribbled by Lee. _____

5. Rachel was accused of traveling by the referee.

   _____

6. The team was congratulated by a teacher. _____

7. Alex was told to shoot the ball by the coach. _____

8. The winners were cheered for by the crowd. _____

Using *be* and *have*

When either **be** or **have** is used as a helping verb, it must agree with the subject.

subject   helping verb   subject   helping verb
He has taken the coaching job, and you and I are learning.

Thinking Questions
Is be *or* have *used as a helping verb? Does it agree with the subject?*

Activity Complete each sentence with the correct form of the verb *be* or *have*. Use the tense shown in parentheses.

1. She _____ feeling good about the game. (past)

2. You and I _____ waiting for the coach. (present)

3. He and I _____ played for two years. (present perfect)

4. You and I _____ going to the game. (future)

5. Tom and the coach _____ talking. (present)

6. He _____ taken the player aside. (present perfect)

7. You _____ seen an improvement. (future)

8. I _____ been to a game here two years ago. (past perfect)

9. Val and Emma _____ becoming basketball fans. (present)

10. I _____ rooting for the team. (present)

Special Subject-Verb Agreement

When a compound subject is joined by *or,*
either…or, or *neither…nor,* the verb agrees with
the subject that is closest to it. When a sentence
begins with *here* or *there,* the verb agrees with
the subject, which comes after the verb.

> **Thinking Questions**
> *If the compound subject of a
> sentence is joined by* or, either...or,
> *or* neither...nor, *does the verb agree
> with the subject that is closest to it?
> If the sentence begins with* here *or*
> there, *does the verb agree with
> the subject of the sentence?*

　　　　　verb　　subject

There <u>are</u> <u>problems</u> with the team, but neither

　　　　　subject　verb

Jason nor <u>Jon</u> <u>has</u> answers.

Activity Write the correct present-tense form of the verb in parentheses.

1. Here (come) the players. _____

2. Neither you nor I (have) played badly. _____

3. There (be) not a boy or a girl here without a team shirt or cap.

   _____

4. Neither the coaches nor José (talk) about it. _____

5. Here (be) Alicia and her brother. _____

6. (Be) you or José leading the team? _____

7. If neither you nor José (play), we'll lose. _____

8. There (go) our last chance. _____

Subordinating Conjunctions

Subordinating Conjunction	**After** we won the basketball game, our team celebrated at the pizza shop.
Independent Clause	After we won the basketball game, **our team celebrated at the pizza shop.**
Dependent Clause	**After we won the basketball game,** our team celebrated at the pizza shop.

1–5.   Circle the subordinating conjunctions. Then write whether each underlined group of words is a *dependent clause* or an *independent clause*.

1. If Pedro makes the free throw, his team will be ahead. _____

2. Although he is not very tall, David plays basketball very well. _____

3. Our team will advance to the playoffs if we win the game today. _____

4. The game will continue until the final buzzer rings. _____

5. Because we scored the most points, our team won the game. _____

6–8.   Combine the simple sentences by using a subordinating conjunction to form a complex sentence.

6. Our team plays at home. Grandma Maria comes to cheer me on.

_____

_____

7. Our family is close and supportive. We gather at each other's games.

_____

_____

8. My family has a big back yard. We hosted the team victory party.

_____

_____

Connect to Writing

Subject-Verb Agreement means that singular subjects need singular verbs, and plural subjects need plural verbs.
Singular Subject and Verb The <u>player wears</u> a uniform.
Plural Subject and Verb George's <u>teammates are</u> loyal.

Change the underlined verb to one that agrees with the subject.

1. He <u>have crammed</u> basketball equipment into his bag. _____

2. She <u>are asking,</u> "What's the score?" _____

3. They <u>is jogging</u> onto the court. _____

4. Everyone <u>have brought</u> a uniform to practice. _____

5. We <u>has had</u> a good game. _____

6. She <u>are becoming</u> an excellent point guard. _____

7. We all <u>agrees</u> the game was tough. _____

8. The sports reporters <u>has taken</u> a lot of pictures. _____

Focus Trait: Purpose
Focusing on Well-Supported Ideas

Any Small Goodness
Writing: Informative Writing

Good writers support their ideas with relevant facts, examples, definitions, and quotations.

This writer deleted a detail that did not provide relevant support and added a strong one.

The animal shelter needs your help. Please consider volunteering a few hours a week. The dogs need to be walked, and the cats need human interaction. ~~Animals enjoy people~~*. The shelter is also in need of office help.* In addition, greeters are needed to talk with visitors ∧about pet adoption.

Read the paragraph. Cross out three details that do not provide strong support. For each one, write a new sentence that provides strong, relevant support for the writer's main idea.

When caring for the shelter cats, please keep the following in mind. The cats are from somewhere else. They may be nervous, so it's important to use calm voices and gentle movements. Always let a cat smell your hand before picking it up. This will help it feel safe. If a cat does not want to be held, put it down. A frightened cat may try to run away. These injuries can be serious. If you are injured by a cat, you'll probably be all right.

1. Old sentence: _____

   New sentence: _____

   _____

2. Old sentence: _____

   New sentence: _____

   _____

3. Old sentence: _____

   New sentence: _____

   _____

 Reader's Guide

Team Moon

Make a Graphic Novel

Graphic novels are not just for superheroes! Use what you have read in "Team Moon" to make pages in a new graphic novel about getting to the moon. In a graphic novel, words and pictures work together to tell a story. How will you help your reader be *right there* at the moon landing?

Look at the moon lander on page 439 and read the quotes on pages 440–441. Some graphic novels include one big picture called a *splash*. It takes up the entire page and focuses on a single event. Choose one or two of the quotes and use pictures and text in a big splash to show what is happening. You may have to reread pages 436–438.

Splash pages are fun to plan and draw, but they are not the only things in a graphic novel.

Read pages 442–445. Use the grid to make a page from a graphic novel that shows what is happening in this section. Add a caption that explains each picture. Remember to use your pictures to convey information such as emotions, time passing, or what it might look like inside mission control. Use information from the text to support your ideas.

Name _____ Date _____

Lesson 15
READER'S NOTEBOOK

Team Moon
Vocabulary Strategies:
Reference Sources

Reference Sources

Find each word in a print or digital dictionary to complete the first two columns of the chart. If the word has more than one part of speech or definition, choose one for the chart. Then use a thesaurus to find a synonym for each word and complete the last column.

Word	Part of Speech	Definition	Synonym
1. apologetic			
2. courtesy			
3. withdraw			
4. expose			
5. flail			
6. vacant			

Now choose two words from the chart and write a sentence for each that uses the meaning you listed.

_____

_____

_____

Name _____ Date _____

Final /ī z/, /ĭ v/, /ĭ j/

Basic Write the Basic Word that best completes each group.

1. tradition, legacy, _____

2. appealing, pleasing, _____

3. change, modify, _____

4. remember, retain, _____

5. certain, definite, _____

6. lack, scarcity, _____

7. publicize, promote, _____

8. university, institute, _____

9. persuade, inspire, _____

10. energetic, lively, _____

11. condense, shorten, _____

12. fitness, workout, _____

13. know, identify, _____

14. sort, group, _____

15. comment, judge, _____

Challenge Imagine you are buying and furnishing a new house.
Write sentences that tell about it. Use three of the Challenge Words.
Write on a separate sheet of paper.

Spelling Words

1. revise
2. advantage
3. memorize
4. active
5. organize
6. criticize
7. shortage
8. advertise
9. attractive
10. college
11. explosive
12. exercise
13. encourage
14. summarize
15. wreckage
16. recognize
17. positive
18. percentage
19. sensitive
20. heritage

Challenge
utilize
mortgage
merchandise
aggressive
compromise

Spelling Word Sort

Write each Basic Word beside the correct heading.

Final /ī z/ spelled -ise	
Final /ī z/ spelled -ize	
Final /ĭ v/ spelled -ive	
Final /ĭ j/ spelled -age	
Other spellings of final /ĭ j/	

Challenge Add the Challenge Words to your Word Sort.

Connect to Reading Look through *Team Moon.* Find words that have the final /ī z/, /ĭ v/, or /ĭ j/ sounds on this page. Add them to your Word Sort.

Spelling Words

1. revise
2. advantage
3. memorize
4. active
5. organize
6. criticize
7. shortage
8. advertise
9. attractive
10. college
11. explosive
12. exercise
13. encourage
14. summarize
15. wreckage
16. recognize
17. positive
18. percentage
19. sensitive
20. heritage

Challenge
utilize
mortgage
merchandise
aggressive
compromise

Name _____ Date _____

Proofreading for Spelling

Find the misspelled words and circle them. Write them correctly on the lines below.

   "Houston, we have a problem." With those chilling words, the Apollo 13 moon mission became a huge rescue effort. A fault in a sensative oxygen tank caused an esplosive problem. NASA engineers scrambled to rivise plans and orginize a way to save the men on the spacecraft. The only advantige NASA had was the cool competence of the men in space. They were activ men who knew the importance of eksercise even in the small capsule. They looked over the wreckige and were able to reckognize the problem they faced. They did not critisize the technicians and maintained a posative attitude, even though there was a shortige of time. They knew their persentage of survival was low. Other astronauts worked to encurage the *Apollo 13* crew.

Spelling Words

1. revise
2. advantage
3. memorize
4. active
5. organize
6. criticize
7. shortage
8. advertise
9. attractive
10. college
11. explosive
12. exercise
13. encourage
14. summarize
15. wreckage
16. recognize
17. positive
18. percentage
19. sensitive
20. heritage

1. _____   8. _____

2. _____   9. _____

3. _____   10. _____

4. _____   11. _____

5. _____   12. _____

6. _____   13. _____

7. _____   14. _____

Name _____ Date _____

Lesson 15
READER'S NOTEBOOK

Team Moon
Grammar: Regular and
Irregular Verbs

Regular and Irregular Verbs

To form the past or past participle of a **regular verb**, the basic rule is to add -*d* or -*ed*. **Irregular verbs** are verbs that do not follow this basic rule.

Thinking Question
To make the past tense of the verb, do you add -d or -ed?

regular verb

My brother and I <u>watched</u> several space shuttle launches on TV.

irregular verb

My brother and I <u>saw</u> many images during the show.

Activity   Write whether the underlined verb is regular or irregular.

1. Twelve people have <u>walked</u> on the moon. _____

2. They all <u>listened</u> to Neil Armstrong. _____

3. On Friday, we <u>left</u> for the moon. _____

4. He <u>loved</u> flying. _____

5. He <u>saw</u> beautiful things in the sky. _____

6. People had never <u>visited</u> the moon before. _____

7. We <u>began</u> to get excited about the journey. _____

8. We <u>spoke</u> about our space adventure. _____

Name _____ Date _____

Lesson 15
READER'S NOTEBOOK

Team Moon
Grammar: Regular and
Irregular Verbs

Common Irregular Verbs

The past and past participle of **irregular verbs** are not formed by adding -d or -ed. Some common irregular verbs are be, go, have, do, see, and eat.

present

The astronauts see Earth from an entirely new perspective.

past

The astronauts saw Earth from an entirely new perspective.

past participle

The astronauts have seen Earth from an entirely new perspective.

Thinking Question
Can you form the past tense of the verb by adding -d or -ed?

Activity Write the past or the past participle of the verb in parentheses to complete the sentence.

1. Many people have _____ to the moon. (go)

2. I _____ a dream last night about being an astronaut. (have)

3. We have _____ images from space for over forty years. (see)

4. They _____ fascinating to look at and learn from. (be)

5. I have never _____ in space. (be)

6. The astronauts _____ into space last month. (go)

7. They _____ food that was specially prepared for space travel. (eat)

8. They _____ Earth from space. (see)

9. Armstrong _____ walk on the moon, marking an important achievement for humans. (do)

10. Space discovery has _____ a great deal of knowledge to our world. (bring)

Irregular Verbs:
Past Tense Form

Irregular verbs do not add –d or –ed in the past tense or past participle.

I <u>told</u> him to look at the rockets.
We <u>drew</u> a picture of the shuttle launch.
Linda <u>chose</u> a book about Mars.
It was cold, so I <u>wore</u> a jacket.

Thinking Question
How is this irregular verb formed in the past tense?

Activity Write the past tense of the irregular verb in parentheses to complete the sentence.

1. The astronauts _____ to the moon. (fly)

2. Armstrong _____ a special suit that enabled him to walk on the moon. (wear)

3. Our parents _____ us about seeing the images on TV. (tell)

4. The astronauts _____ space travel very seriously. (take)

5. They _____ in a ship powered by a rocket. (ride)

6. The crew _____ moon rocks back to Earth. (bring)

7. Maria once _____ of becoming an astronaut. (think)

8. I _____ an awesome picture of the shuttle. (draw)

9. We _____ to talk about space travel in class. (choose)

10. Marc _____ a report on the topic. (write)

Name _____ Date _____

Longer Sentences

Simple	Neil is an astronaut.
Compound	Neil is an astronaut, and he travels to space.
Complex	Since traveling to space is dangerous, Neil trains for many months.
Compound-Complex	Until the next mission takes place, Neil will train rigorously, and he will focus on his duties as an astronaut.

1–6. For each sentence, write *simple, compound, complex,* or *compound-complex.* Add missing commas.

1. The rockets fired and the shuttle blasted off into space.

   _____

2. After the shuttle left the atmosphere the boosters detached and the

   shuttle orbited the earth. _____

3. The spacecraft soared into space. _____

4. We floated around the cabin because there is no gravity in space.

   _____

5. Although outer space is cold the astronauts stay warm inside the

   shuttle and they wear shorts and T-shirts. _____

6. The crew will conduct scientific experiments. _____

7–8. Rewrite the sentences to form compound-complex sentences.

7. Outer space is a vacuum. There is no air. It is very cold.

   _____

   _____

8. Humans have traveled to space for decades. We still have much to

   learn about the universe. We will continue to explore outer space.

   _____

   _____

Connect to Writing

When you write, it is important to use **exact verbs**. A weak verb does not show action as clearly as an exact verb.
Weak Verb   The boy <u>got</u> here late.
Exact Verb   The boy <u>arrived</u> here late.

Write an exact verb to replace the underlined verb.

1. The astronauts <u>looked</u> through the window. _____

2. The moon <u>was</u> ahead. _____

3. Armstrong <u>went</u> down the ladder of the lunar module. _____

4. He <u>walked</u> on the surface of the moon. _____

5. The scientists <u>talked</u> excitedly. _____

6. They all <u>watched</u> his legendary excursion. _____

7. The astronauts <u>got</u> soil and rock samples from the moon's surface. _____

8. They <u>put</u> an American flag on the moon. _____

Focus Trait: Elaboration
Creating Voice in a Formal Style

Sentences	Formal Sentences with Emotion
The space museum has lots of cool things to see from a real space mission to the moon. You can also look at a moon buggy used by astronauts on their mission.	The exhibit at the space museum provides an incredible variety of authentic items from a lunar space mission. Visitors stand in awe and amazement as they view the lunar roving vehicle that once transported astronauts on the moon.

A. Read the passage below. Underline the sentences that express the writer's personality and emotion.

> The moon's surface was in sight now. Slowly, slowly . . . then finally! The Eagle came to its resting place on the Sea of Tranquility. But did the crew land on a body of water?
>
> No, the Sea of Tranquility is not a body of water. It is the surface area where the Apollo 11 crew landed their lunar module.
>
> The moon's surface is dense with craters. No wonder it is often compared to cheese! The Apollo 11 crew needed to find a smooth surface area, and the Sea of Tranquility provided optimal landing conditions.
>
> The Sea of Tranquility wasn't completely crater-free, though. The Apollo 11 crew had to maneuver their way around a crater rim before they could breathe a sigh of relief.

Pair/Share Work with a partner to brainstorm how to revise each sentence to express emotion while maintaining a formal writing style. Write the new sentences on a separate sheet of paper.

1. The astronauts walked through moon dust.

2. The moon buggy shot across the surface.

3. The temperature in the capsule was too cold.

4. The astronauts picked up moon rocks to take home.

Reader's Guide

The Real Vikings

An Archaeologist for a Day

You have been asked to join the archaeological dig at Hedeby. Archaeologists sketch what they find and label everything in their sketches. Labels should include a description of the item, where it was found, and what it might be used for.

Read pages 470–473. Document a house that has been found at Hedeby. Use what you have read to show what was found at the dig. Label your findings with information from the text. At the bottom of the sketch, write a conclusion about the building you have found. Base this conclusion on the artifacts at the site.

Congratulations, you made a find of your own! You found the grave of the young Viking man whose boast you read about on page 475. Write about your find.

Read pages 468–469 and 474. Sketch your find. Label what you found in the same way that you sketched the building you worked on earlier. At the bottom, write a statement about what kind of life the young man lived. Was he married? a farmer? a fisherman? Use what you have found to support your ideas.

Name _____ Date _____

Lesson 16
READER'S NOTEBOOK

The Real Vikings
Vocabulary Strategies:
Greek Roots

Greek Roots

The words below are formed using one of the following roots: *geo*, meaning "earth," *graph*, meaning "write," *therm*, meaning "heat," *hydra*, meaning "water," *tele*, meaning "distance," or *opt*, meaning "eye." Choose the word from the box that best completes each sentence. Then use your own words to define the word.

telegraph   geography   thermometer
hydrated   optical   telescope

1. We used a _____ to view the constellations in the night sky.

_____

2. Students learn about the world's different countries in _____ class.

_____

3. Before the invention of the telephone, people use a _____ to communicate over long distances.

_____

4. The accident injured his _____ nerve, interfering with his vision.

_____

5. It is important to keep your body _____. by drinking a lot of water.

_____

6. Jaime's mother took her temperature using a _____.

_____

Suffixes: -ent, -ant

Basic Write the Basic Words that best fit the spaces in each sentence pair.

1–2. Mom could sense my _____ and hesitation before the art show. I was always _____ to show my art to other people.

3–4. Mom always says that I need to build my _____. I've never been that _____ in my drawings.

5–6. My friend Steve is a _____ artist. It's easy to be envious of his _____.

7–8. I felt a little better when my classmates said that my art was _____. Maybe they are just practicing common _____.

9–10. Wow! I was awarded a first-place ribbon for _____. This has turned out to be an _____ day!

11–12. I didn't want my pride to be too _____, so I kept my thoughts to myself, but my enormous smile was _____ of how happy I was.

Challenge Write a paragraph about a family outing on a lake. Use the four Challenge Words. Write on a separate sheet of paper.

Spelling Words

1. confident
2. confidence
3. fragrant
4. fragrance
5. excellent
6. excellence
7. decent
8. decency
9. truant
10. truancy
11. brilliant
12. brilliance
13. resident
14. residence
15. evident
16. evidence
17. occupant
18. occupancy
19. reluctant
20. reluctance

Challenge
inconvenient
inconvenience
buoyant
buoyancy

Spelling Word Sort

Write each Basic Word beside the correct heading.

-ent	
-ant	
-ence, -ency	
-ance, -ancy	

Challenge   Add the Challenge Words to your Word Sort.

Spelling Words

1. confident
2. confidence
3. fragrant
4. fragrance
5. excellent
6. excellence
7. decent
8. decency
9. truant
10. truancy
11. brilliant
12. brilliance
13. resident
14. residence
15. evident
16. evidence
17. occupant
18. occupancy
19. reluctant
20. reluctance

Challenge
inconvenient
inconvenience
buoyant
buoyancy

Name _____ Date _____

Proofreading for Spelling

Find the misspelled words and circle them. Write them correctly on the lines below.

How did the Vikings come to dominate most shipping and trade? The evadent answer is the eksellence of their ships. Their longships made it possible for them to take up residance even in North America. Also, many a Viking became an ocupent of Iceland. They were able to trade for fragrent spices and take occupancy of other lands with ease. Never ones to be truent from a battle, the fierce crews of the warships sailed wherever they wished—and no residant of a coastal area was safe.

Yet much evidence shows that trade was as important to the Vikings as conquest. The key was their exsellent ships, made of split oak wood. Just imagine the fragrince of the shipyards! Imagine the noise and activity! Imagine, too, how these harsh warriors dealt with truansy among the workers.

Spelling Words

1. confident
2. confidence
3. fragrant
4. fragrance
5. excellent
6. excellence
7. decent
8. decency
9. truant
10. truancy
11. brilliant
12. brilliance
13. resident
14. residence
15. evident
16. evidence
17. occupant
18. occupancy
19. reluctant
20. reluctance

1. _____   7. _____
2. _____   8. _____
3. _____   9. _____
4. _____   10. _____
5. _____   11. _____
6. _____   12. _____

Principal Parts of Verbs

Verbs have four basic forms, or **principal parts**: present, past, present participle, and past participle. For regular verbs, the past tense is formed by adding -ed to the present tense. The present participle is the -ing form of the verb that is used with the helping verb to be. The past participle is usually formed the same as the past tense and is used with the helping verbs to have and to be.

present tense
I work hard every day.

past tense
I worked late last night.

present participle
I am working right now.

past participle
I have worked all my life.

Thinking Question
Which principal part of the verb fits the context of this sentence?

Activity Write the correct form of the verb on the line. Then tell whether the verb tense is *present, past, present participle,* or *past participle.*

1. The archaeologist _____ all day. (dig) _____

2. We _____ new facts during last week's trip. (discover)
   _____

3. I'm _____ a career in history. (consider)
   _____

4. We _____ something new every day. (learn) _____

5. Jordan _____ every artifact that was found. (list) _____

6. Yesterday, the teacher _____ us where to look. (tell) _____

7. The archaeologists have _____ so many facts. (memorize)
   _____

Name _____ Date _____

Lesson 16
READER'S NOTEBOOK

The Real Vikings
Grammar: Principal Parts
of Verbs

Principal Parts of Irregular Verbs

The **past** and **past participle** of irregular verbs are not formed by adding an -*ed*, as with regular verbs. The principal parts of these verbs must be memorized. Some common irregular verbs include: *eat, see, go, have,* and *be.*

Irregular verb using past participle

I haven't <u>eaten</u> since breakfast.

Thinking Question
How are the past and past participle of irregular verbs formed?

Activity Write the past or the past participle of the verb in parentheses to complete the sentence.

1. The Vikings _____ to a variety of countries. (go)

2. We haven't _____ anything like it. (see)

3. They _____ many prisoners. (catch)

4. We have _____ far to see the exhibit. (drive)

5. The Vikings _____ many ships. (build)

6. We _____ the last ones to leave the museum. (be)

7. We had _____ to listen to the lecture. (choose)

8. I _____ an expert on Vikings. (become)

Name _____ Date _____

Lesson 16
READER'S NOTEBOOK

The Real Vikings
Grammar: Principal Parts
of Verbs

Using Consistent Tenses

When you write, it is important to use **consistent tenses**. Tense refers to time. In writing, all verbs in a sentence or paragraph should usually be in the same tense: past, present, or future.

Inconsistent tense

The cat <u>ran</u> outside and <u>climbs</u> the tree.

Consistent tense

The cat <u>ran</u> outside and <u>climbed</u> the tree.

Thinking Question
Are all the verbs in the sentence written in the same tense?

Activity Write the correct form of the verb in parentheses on the line.

1. The Vikings stole from people and _____ what was not theirs. (take)

2. Tom will read about the Vikings, and then he _____ a summary. (write)

3. Yesterday, I learned about pirates and _____ my sister all about them. (tell)

4. Even today, people _____ and learn about the lives of pirates. (study)

5. The "Golden Age of Piracy" _____ in the early 1600s and ended in the 1700s. (start)

6. The Vikings _____ excellent ships and had many battles. (sail)

7. They _____ Old Norse and lived in Scandinavia. (speak)

8. Tomorrow, we _____ more about Vikings, and Tara will give a presentation. (learn)

Kinds of Pronouns

Kinds of Pronouns	Examples
Subject Pronouns	**He** was a famous warrior.
Object Pronouns	The crew's stories amazed **us**.
Possessive Pronouns	**Her** poster has colorful pictures of famous ships. The best poster was **ours**.

1–6. Circle the correct pronouns.

1. Ann wrote a poem about the warrior, but (her, she) did not read (him, it) in class.

2. (My, Mine) report on the Vikings is longer than (your, you're) report.

3. (It's, Its) an interesting report, but (it's, its) introduction needs work.

4. As a result of the last raid, many villagers lost (their, they're) homes.

5. The warriors had a bad reputation, but (they, them) were not all cruel.

6. Egil Skallagrimmson was a famous merchant, and (he, him) was also a poet.

7–8. Combine each pair of sentences using the subordinating conjunction in parentheses. Replace one subject with the correct pronoun. Be sure to avoid vague pronouns.

7. The archaeologists dug up the artifacts. The archaeologists were able to form a truer picture of ancient life in Kenya. (after)

_____

_____

8. Most homes had no windows. The homes were probably very dark inside. (because)

_____

_____

Connect to Writing

Participles can be used to describe nouns. Good writers sometimes combine sentences by using participles as describing words.

Two sentences	Combined sentence
The museum has been <u>crowded</u> since the doors opened. The museum is packed with groups of schoolchildren.	The <u>crowded</u> museum has been packed with groups of schoolchildren since the doors opened.

Combine the two sentences. Use the underlined participle to describe the noun in the new sentence.

1. The village had been <u>abandoned</u>. The village was silent as a grave.

   _____

   _____

2. The news is <u>encouraging</u>. The news makes the Viking elders smile.

   _____

   _____

3. The water was <u>rushing</u> over the banks. The water flooded the village.

   _____

   _____

4. The boys have been <u>sprinting</u> across the field. The boys are catching the horses.

   _____

   _____

5. The fans were <u>booing</u>. They had been cheering for their favorite players.

   _____

   _____

Focus Trait: Elaboration
Standard English

Instead of this . . .	the author wrote this:
Life was **tough** in Viking days—but **for certain**, there was still time to **kick back** and **chill**.	Life was hard in Viking times—but there was obviously still time to relax and have fun. (p. 475)

List the nonstandard words and phrases in the sentences below.

	Nonstandard Words and Phrases
1. My brother kept bugging me to loan him my snowshoes, but I told him to knock it off. 2. Roasting meat on the spit was a nightmare, but my old man kept his cool.	_____ _____ _____ _____ _____ _____ _____

Pair/Share Work with a partner to identify the nonstandard English words and phrases and rewrite the sentences in standard English.

	Standard English
3. Ava had to get up at the crack of dawn because the rug she was weaving was a doozy. 4. I was stumped by crocheting, but I gave it another shot. 5. We split after we blew all our coins on some cheezy beads at the fair. 6. We were majorly hungry, so we scarfed down all the bread and stew.	_____ _____ _____ _____ _____ _____ _____ _____

Name _____ Date _____

Lesson 17
READER'S NOTEBOOK

The Emperor's
Silent Army
Independent Reading

 Reader's Guide

The Emperor's Silent Army

Create a Museum Plaque

You are a museum curator. You have been asked to create a series of plaques that explain the terra cotta warrior display. For each claim you make, support it with factual evidence from the text. Remember, not all the claims made by the author may be based on facts.

Read the last paragraph on page 499, all of page 500, and the first paragraph on page 501. Write an explanation to help museum visitors understand the purpose of the terra cotta warriors.

Claim: _____

_____

_____

_____

_____

Title: _____

_____

_____

_____

_____

Description: _____

_____

_____

_____

_____

Name _____ Date _____

Lesson 17
READER'S NOTEBOOK

The Emperor's
Silent Army
Independent Reading

Read the second, third, and fourth paragraphs on page 501 and all of page 502. Write an explanation to help museum visitors understand how the terra cotta warriors were constructed.

Claim: _____

Title: _____

_____

_____

_____

_____

_____

_____

_____

_____

Description: _____

_____

_____

_____

_____

_____

_____

Word Families

The words in the box are part of one of three word families, related by the roots *hydro/hydra/hydr* ("water") and *magna* ("great" or large"), and the base word "possess." Choose the word from the box that best completes each sentence.

magnificent	dehydrated	possessor
magnify	hydroelectric	possessive

1. The Emperor was the _____ of many kingdoms and riches.

2. We had to _____ the text on the computer screen because it was too small to read.

3. The dam is _____, using water to help generate electricity.

Use the remaining words to create three new sentences.

4. _____

_____

5. _____

_____

6. _____

_____

Suffixes: *-able, -ible, -ate*

Basic Write the Basic Word that has a similar meaning.

1. lucky
2. very unhappy
3. to finish a course of study
4. amazing
5. loud enough to be heard
6. apparent
7. thoughtful of others
8. fragile
9. work together
10. terrible
11. capable of being cleaned in water

1. _____   7. _____
2. _____   8. _____
3. _____   9. _____
4. _____   10. _____
5. _____   11. _____
6. _____

Challenge Think about the features of tall tales. Write a paragraph about tall tales. Use three of the Challenge Words. Write on a separate sheet of paper.

Spelling Words

1. visible
2. enjoyable
3. celebrate
4. incredible
5. horrible
6. desperate
7. cooperate
8. valuable
9. appreciate
10. considerate
11. audible
12. delicate
13. washable
14. graduate
15. capable
16. miserable
17. sensible
18. fortunate
19. noticeable
20. responsible

Challenge
evacuate
irritable
exaggerate
improbable
elaborate

Spelling Word Sort

Write each Basic Word beside the correct heading.

-able	
-ible	
-ate	

Spelling Words

1. visible
2. enjoyable
3. celebrate
4. incredible
5. horrible
6. desperate
7. cooperate
8. valuable
9. appreciate
10. considerate
11. audible
12. delicate
13. washable
14. graduate
15. capable
16. miserable
17. sensible
18. fortunate
19. noticeable
20. responsible

Challenge
evacuate
irritable
exaggerate
improbable
elaborate

Challenge   Add the Challenge Words to your Word Sort.

Connect to Reading   Look through *The Emperor's Silent Army*. Find words that have the suffixes *-able, -ible,* and *-ate*. Add them to your Word Sort.

Proofreading for Spelling

Find the misspelled words and circle them. Write them correctly on the lines below.

There is almost an art to uncovering troves of ancient treasures. Usually, little is visibel aboveground. Because archaeologists always apreshiate how valuible their finds may be, digging around ancient artworks requires a sensable approach. Only responsable, capible people do the delacite work of cleaning away centuries of dirt and debris. Some people celibrait the task, finding the extremely careful work enjoyible. Others consider it a tedious chore. Either way, it must be done with incredable care. Heavy machinery is used only under the most desperite circumstances, such as if the archaeologists are required to work very quickly for some reason. If they are fotunite, they manage to preserve the art even under those conditions.

Spelling Words
1. visible
2. enjoyable
3. celebrate
4. incredible
5. horrible
6. desperate
7. cooperate
8. valuable
9. appreciate
10. considerate
11. audible
12. delicate
13. washable
14. graduate
15. capable
16. miserable
17. sensible
18. fortunate
19. noticeable
20. responsible

1. _____   7. _____

2. _____   8. _____

3. _____   9. _____

4. _____   10. _____

5. _____   11. _____

6. _____   12. _____

Demonstrative and Indefinite Pronouns

A **demonstrative pronoun** points out a specific person, place, or thing. Demonstrative pronouns are *this*, *that*, *these*, and *those*. An **indefinite pronoun** points to something that is not specific. Some indefinite pronouns are *all*, *another*, *any*, *each*, *everyone*, *someone*, and *none*.

demonstrative pronoun
This is my favorite class.

indefinite pronoun
Each of the students must write a report.

Thinking Question
Does the pronoun point to something specific or nonspecific?

Activity Complete each sentence with a demonstrative or an indefinite pronoun.

1. _____ is the best book about emperors.

2. What should I do with _____ other books?

3. Not just _____ can be an emperor.

4. _____ of the books should be returned to the library.

5. The teacher said that _____ book has its own spot.

6. _____ found this fact, but I'm not sure who.

7. _____ were pretty tough emperors back then.

8. They conquered _____ of the territories they set their sights on.

Interrogative Pronouns

An **interrogative pronoun** is a pronoun that asks a question. Interrogative pronouns are: *who, whom, which, what,* and *whose.*

interrogative pronoun
What is the capital of modern China?

Thinking Question
Does the pronoun ask a question?

Activity Underline the interrogative pronoun in each sentence.

1. Which of these vases do you like best?
2. Who is the president of China?
3. For whom was this palace built?
4. Whose beautiful Chinese chess set is this?
5. What is the meaning of this carved inscription?
6. Who wants to come to the museum?
7. What can I buy for fifty yuan?
8. Whose are these chopsticks lying on the floor?

Reflexive and Intensive Pronouns

A **reflexive pronoun** is a pronoun that refers to a noun or pronoun in the sentence. It ends in *-self* or *-selves* and cannot be taken out without changing the meaning of the sentence. An **intensive pronoun** ends in *-self* or *-selves* and emphasizes a noun or pronoun. It can be taken out without changing the meaning of the sentence.

Thinking Questions
Does the pronoun end in -self or -selves? Does it refer to or emphasize a noun or pronoun? Can it be taken out without changing the meaning of the sentence?

reflexive pronoun
Una made <u>herself</u> a sandwich for lunch.

intensive pronoun
I was hungry <u>myself</u>, so I made a sandwich, too.

Activity Underline the reflexive or intensive pronoun in each sentence. Write *reflexive* or *intensive* on the line.

1. We gave ourselves time to visit the site. _____
2. The emperor surrounded himself with servants. _____
3. Beijing does not itself lie on the sea, but nearby Tianjin does. _____
4. We helped ourselves to more noodles. _____
5. The emperor himself dresses in silk from my shop. _____
6. I asked myself why I had never been to China. _____
7. China sees itself as a great world power. _____
8. What do you think about that yourself? _____

Simple Verb Tenses

Present tense	Jan **looks** for a book about Chinese mythology.
Past tense	She **looked** in the library yesterday.
Future tense	She will **look** at an online bookstore tomorrow.

1–6. **Write the correct form of the verb in parentheses on the line.**

1. Long ago, people _____ their beliefs about life and nature through myths. (express)

2. In the West today, people mostly _____ Greek and Roman myths. (know)

3. Ancient China _____ many exciting stories about gods and goddesses as well. (produce)

4. These stories _____ ancient peoples about the consequences of bad behavior. (warn)

5. My cousin _____ Chinese myths so English speakers can learn them. (translate)

6. People _____ these myths for years to come. (enjoy)

7–12. **This journal entry has six errors in verb tense. Use proofreading marks to correct the entry.**

I am reading a collection of Chinese legends for my English report. So far, I will like the stories with Monkey as the main character the best. Mrs. Sturgis assigns the report last month. She said we could prepare a written report or an oral report. Then she ask us our preference. I decide on an oral report. Next Monday, I present my report in front of the class. Now, my friend Anita wished her report was oral, too.

Connect to Writing

Noun Overload	The artifacts attracted visitors from all over the world. People came especially to see the artifacts.
Repeated Nouns Replaced with Pronouns	The artifacts attracted visitors from all over the world. People came especially to see them.

1–3. Replace the underlined noun with a pronoun.

1. The tour bus left without the students. _____

2. Kim and Benny did not want the trip to end. _____

3. Ms. Jenson taught us about ancient life and culture. _____

4–6. Add pronouns to avoid repetition. Combine sentences if it makes sense to do so. Write the new sentence on the line.

4. The students studied and worked hard. The students got to know each other well and learned to work together as a team.

_____

_____

5. The people of Qin were known for their fierceness. Their fierceness was the reason Qin conquered the other kingdoms.

_____

_____

6. The other kingdoms fought well. The kingdom of Qin still conquered the other kingdoms.

_____

_____

The Emperor's
Silent Army
Writing: Informative Writing

Focus Trait: Organization
Offer Solutions

> Good writers organize a problem-solution essay by discussing problems first and then solutions and by grouping appropriate details with the problem and with the solution.
>
> *Visitors to Xian, China, can't see the terracotta warriors as they originally appeared. Many of the figures have broken into pieces. Also, when the figures are dug up, most of their paint peels off. The solution is to create replicas of the soldiers. Artisans can copy the size and shape of the original sculptures. In addition, they can use any paint chips they find to make computer images that will help them color the replicas. The result may not be as authentic as the original, but it's still valuable.*

Read the list of details below. Then group them with the problem or the solution in an order that makes sense.

Details: They drive a cart of smelly fish in front of the dead man's chariot to hide the stench. He and his court are far from the capital. They carry out daily routines as if the emperor were alive. His ministers fear a revolt in the capital if the news gets out.

Problem: Emperor Qin Shihuang dies while on a trip.	**Solution:** His ministers hide the fact until his body can be returned to the capital.
Details:	**Details:**
_____	_____
_____	_____
_____	_____
_____	_____

Name _____ Date _____

Lesson 18
READER'S NOTEBOOK

The Hero and the Minotaur
Independent Reading

The Hero and the Minotaur

Write a Newspaper Article

Suppose you lived in Athens. You are assigned to write
a series of newspaper articles to tell about Theseus' adventure.
Use examples from the text to show how Theseus responds
to the challenges he faces.

**Read page 525. Describe how the plot unfolds in this passage and
how Theseus responds. Use a catchy headline to capture the action
in this article.**

_____

Athens

_____

_____

_____

_____

_____

_____

_____

_____

Read page 528 and the first paragraph on page 529.
Write an article about the experience and include a headline.

Crete

_____

_____

_____

_____

_____

_____

Read the second and third paragraphs on page 529, and all of pages 531 and 532. Write an article about the experience and include a headline.

Crete

_____

_____

_____

_____

_____

_____

Lesson 18
READER'S NOTEBOOK

**The Hero and
the Minotaur**
Vocabulary Strategies: Suffixes
-ful, -less, -ly, -ness, -ment, -ship

Suffixes *-ful, -less, -ly, -ness, -ment, -ship*

The words in the box end with a suffix that means "in a <u>certain</u> way,"
"full of," "without," or "the state or quality of being." Choose a word from the
box that best completes each sentence. Then create a definition for the word,
based on the meaning of its suffix and base word.

> hardship   eagerly   happiness   secretly   embarrassment
> dutiful   sorrowful   joyless   friendship   pointless

1. The family faced much financial _____ when both parents lost
   their jobs. _____

2. She showed her _____ when she helped Jessica finish her
   chores. _____

3. The gift was given _____ so the receiver could not directly
   thank the giver. _____

4. To be filled with sadness is to feel _____. _____

5. The dog watched _____ as its master filled the bowl with
   food. _____

6. Spending Saturday afternoon indoors was a _____ occasion.
   _____

7. I felt such _____ when I found out I had won first place in the
   contest. _____

8. It was a great _____ to the class when no one passed the
   exam. _____

9. It was _____ to continue searching for the lost key in the dark.
   _____

10. _____ children clean up after themselves. _____

Name _____ Date _____

Spelling /sh/

Basic Complete the puzzle by writing the Basic Word for each clue.

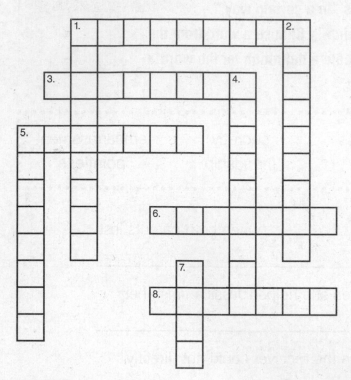

Across

1. tastes very good
3. Is the tire inflated to the correct _____?
5. very old
6. the opposite of deep
8. shy

Down

1. general line you are moving in
2. The police said the _____ was under control.
4. to create or set up
5. surprise
7. acting without careful consideration

Spelling Words

1. section
2. shallow
3. direction
4. musician
5. rash
6. position
7. astonish
8. pressure
9. attention
10. impression
11. crucial
12. official
13. emotion
14. bashful
15. delicious
16. establish
17. ancient
18. situation
19. suspicion
20. permission

Challenge
diminish
beneficial
efficient
potential
compassion

Challenge Come up with an idea for a new charity. What will your charity do? Whom will it try to help? Write a description of your new charity. Use four of the Challenge Words. Write on a separate sheet of paper.

Spelling Word Sort

Write each Basic Word beside the correct heading.

/sh/ spelled *sh*	
/sh/ spelled *ti*	
/sh/ spelled *ci*	
/sh/ spelled *ss*	

Challenge Add the Challenge Words to your Word Sort.

Connect to Reading Look through *The Hero and the Minotaur.* Find words that have the /sh/ spelling patterns on this page. Add them to your Word Sort.

Spelling Words

1. section
2. shallow
3. direction
4. musician
5. rash
6. position
7. astonish
8. pressure
9. attention
10. impression
11. crucial
12. official
13. emotion
14. bashful
15. delicious
16. establish
17. ancient
18. situation
19. suspicion
20. permission

Challenge
diminish
beneficial
efficient
potential
compassion

Proofreading for Spelling

The Hero and the Minotaur

Spelling: Spelling /sh/

Find the misspelled words and circle them. Write them correctly on the lines below.

Greenview Middle School's production of *The Minotaur* held its oficial opening night tonight. Under the direshion of Ms. Linda Steers, the cast brings this aincient tale to life in an exciting new way. Josh Ballard plays the lead role in this musical, and shows both his talent as a musishan and his ability to handle the prescure of the leading role. He is neither bashfful nor racsh, and shows just the right emoshion to make his character come to life on the stage. Much attencion has been paid to the details in the stage design, which works to establicsh the crushial setting in the labyrinth. The cast and crew will continue to astonicsh audiences through next Sunday, when the show closes. Seats are still available in almost any secstion. Be sure to ask your parents' permicion to attend. This is a show you don't want to miss!

Spelling Words

1. section
2. shallow
3. direction
4. musician
5. rash
6. position
7. astonish
8. pressure
9. attention
10. impression
11. crucial
12. official
13. emotion
14. bashful
15. delicious
16. establish
17. ancient
18. situation
19. suspicion
20. permission

1. _____   8. _____
2. _____   9. _____
3. _____   10. _____
4. _____   11. _____
5. _____   12. _____
6. _____   13. _____
7. _____   14. _____

Adjectives and Adverbs

Adjectives modify nouns and pronouns, while **adverbs** modify verbs, adjectives, and other adverbs.

Adjective   **adverb**
The <u>red</u> sun blazed <u>fiercely</u> on the ancient ruins.

Thinking Questions
Does the word modify a noun or a pronoun? Does the word modify a verb, an adjective, or an adverb?

1–5.   Underline the adjectives.

1. This king was extremely cruel.

2. The Aegean Sea is vast and very deep.

3. Minotaurs are often quite unfriendly.

4. It is nearly always sunny in Greece.

5. Greece has a fairly long coastline.

6–10.   Underline the adverbs.

6. This king was extremely cruel.

7. The Aegean Sea is vast and very deep.

8. Minotaurs are often quite unfriendly.

9. It is nearly always sunny in Greece.

10. Greece has a fairly long coastline.

Articles and Demonstratives

The **definite article** *the* is used before a noun that refers to a specific person, place, or thing. The **indefinite articles** *a* and *an* are used before nouns that refer to any person, place, or thing. The **demonstratives** – *this*, *that*, *these*, and *those* – show where something is.
This and *these* indicate that something is nearby.
That and *those* indicate that something is far away.

Thinking Questions
Does the noun refer to something specific or not specific? Does it refer to something nearby or far away?

definite	indefinite	indefinite

<u>The</u> trip is long. <u>A</u> trip can be long. <u>An</u> adventure can be dangerous.

demonstratives

I always visit <u>this</u> island. Do you want to visit <u>that</u> island?
I always use <u>these</u> maps. Can you hand me <u>those</u> maps?

Activity Circle the correct article or demonstrative in parentheses.

1. Did you like (these, those) pita chips we had at the party?

2. We visited (the, a) Parthenon yesterday.

3. It's exciting to see (these, this) ruins close up.

4. I can't reach (this, that) guidebook. It's too high on the shelf.

5. Overall, it has been (the, an) educational trip.

6. (This, that) Greek artifact in my hand is ancient.

7. Can you hand me (a, the) travel brochure from the pile?

8. Use binoculars to see (this, that) ancient ruin.

Proper Adjectives

A **proper adjective** starts with a capital letter and refers to a specific person, place, or thing. A **common adjective** does not refer to a specific person, place, or thing, and does not start with a capital letter.

proper adjective
I met a nice <u>American</u> woman on my trip.

common adjective
I met a <u>nice</u> American woman on my trip.

Thinking Question
Does the adjective start with a capital letter and refer to a specific person, place, or thing?

Activity   Write whether the underlined adjective is proper or common.

1. We saw many <u>breathtaking</u> sites on the trip. _____

2. I enjoyed learning about <u>Greek</u> culture. _____

3. My new friend wanted to practice speaking the <u>English</u> language.

   _____

4. The ancient architecture was <u>beautiful</u>. _____

5. Mary said she would like to go to a <u>Cretan</u> restaurant. _____

6. Ancient Greece was ruled by <u>wealthy</u> landowners. _____

7. The Greeks were very powerful during the <u>Hellenistic</u> period.

   _____

Correct Pronouns

Possessive Pronoun Examples
<u>His</u> father sent him to fight the Minotaur.
That baklava is <u>hers</u>.
<u>Whose</u> vacation was better?
Consistent Pronouns
People enjoy myths for many reasons. <u>They</u> read <u>them</u> to learn lessons about the world, and <u>they</u> learn about the lives of ancient peoples.

1–8.   Underline the possessive pronouns in parentheses to complete the sentences.

1. The book about Greece was (hers, she).

2. (His, Him) heart was beating fast when he faced (his, him) enemy.

3. This passport is (mine, I), and that one is (your's, yours).

4. (Their, There) room has a better view of the Parthenon.

5. When we order our Greek salads, how do you want (yours, your's)?

6. (Who's, Whose) vacation was more fun?

7. (She, Her) camera is full of pictures from the trip.

8. The idea for this whole trip was (mine, my).

9–13.   This writer's journal entry has five errors in pronoun consistency. Use proofreading marks to correct the entry.

I don't know why some people think they don't like myths. It

is great! We tell about great adventures and strange, far-away lands.

Heroes perform feats of strength and save his people.

I think if you just read some myths, they would change your minds!

Connect to Writing

When you write, it is important to use precise adjectives and adverbs to describe nouns or verbs. A precise adjective or adverb provides an exact description as opposed to a vague one.

Less precise adjective

The Minotaur was <u>mean</u>.

More precise adjective

The Minotaur was <u>vicious</u>.

Write whether the underlined adjective or adverb is precise or not precise.

1. Greek myths are <u>nice</u> stories. _____

2. The stories are <u>fictional</u>. _____

3. Most Greeks have a <u>profound</u> respect for tradition. _____

4. The rock outcrops and beaches of the Cycladic Islands are <u>beautiful</u>. _____

5. The tour bus went <u>really</u> fast. _____

6. She fought <u>courageously</u> to keep the island safe. _____

7. The islands are <u>rugged</u>. _____

8. It was a <u>very</u> hot day. _____

Focus Trait: Organization
Transitions

Good writers use transition words and phrases in their writing. Transitions make writing more coherent and therefore easier to understand. Transition words and phrases can bridge the gap between two different ideas, show contrast, or sum up ideas. Some commonly used transition words and phrases are *also, additionally, as a result, because, besides that, consequently, first, finally, instead of, on the other hand, second, since, so,* and *then.*

Rewrite the following paragraph, using transition words and phrases to make the writing easier to understand.

In Greek mythology, the word *Minotaur* means "Minos' bull." The word comes from the proper noun, Minos. It is capitalized. The creature was known by its individual name, Asterion. Some sources say the Minotaur had the body of a man and the head of a bull. Others say it had a man's head and a bull's body. The Minotaur was extremely vicious. Minos had Daedelus build the Labyrinth to hold it. Many people have looked for the possible site of the Labyrinth. Some say it was in Minos' palace in Knossos. The palace is a maze-like collection of rooms. The Labyrinth could be somewhere near the palace.

Name _____ Date _____

Lesson 19
READER'S NOTEBOOK

The Princess Who
Became a King
Independent Reading

 Reader's Guide

The Princess Who Became a King

Write an Interview

Hatshepsut led an interesting life. Suppose you had the chance to interview her. What would she say? Use text evidence from the passages to write responses to these interview questions.

Read page 557 and the first paragraph of page 558 to answer the interviewer's question.

Interviewer: Some say that your carefree days at the palace ended when you became a teenager. How is this true?

Hatshepsut:

_____

_____

_____

_____

_____

_____

Name _____ Date _____

Read the first and second paragraphs on page 559. Use textual evidence to support your response to this question.

Interviewer: You soon became the Queen Regent. Did it seem as if the gods had intervened in your life?

Hatshepsut:

_____

_____

_____

_____

Read the first and second paragraphs on page 561. Use textual evidence to support your response to this question.

Interviewer: Some say that you were confident, smart, and fearless. Do you agree?

Hatshepsut:

_____

_____

_____

_____

Greek Roots & Affixes

The words below are formed from Greek roots or affixes. Choose the word from the box that best completes each sentence. Then use the context in which the word is used and what you know about the word parts to determine the meaning.

> synthesis   recycle   biography   cyclist
> tricycle   synchronize   sympathy   biodiversity

1. The _____ rode for 100 miles and broke a world record. _____

2. Costa Rica is a country with a lot of _____, in that there are many different kinds of plants and animals there. _____ _____

3. We had to _____ our watches so they all told the same time. _____

4. The toddler rode a _____, which was safer because it had three wheels. _____

5. I had _____ for the girl who lost her brand-new kitten. _____

6. It's better for the environment if you _____ paper instead of throwing it in the trash. _____

7. I read a _____ about the poet Emily Dickinson. _____

8. We made a _____ of our ideas by combining them into one summary. _____

Plurals

Basic Read the paragraph. Write the Basic Words that best complete the sentences.

The (1) were falling off the trees as we drove toward the farm. "Are there (2) in the woods?" Jimmy asked. "No," my mother said, "there's nothing dangerous in the woods."

When we arrived, Grandpa gave us a tour. He explained how the (3) of the different crops he grew changed every year. When he showed us the barn, Jimmy and I screamed to see if we could hear (4) of our voices. "Boys! Behave (5) around the animals!" Grandpa said, pointing to a pair of (6). "They're too young for all that noise." Then he took Jimmy and me up to the hayloft. He said we could play there if we were careful. We walked along the edge pretending we were (7) chasing a group of dangerous bandits along high (8).

That night we had roast beef with (9) that came from Grandma's garden, and a salad topped with (10) picked right off the vine. It was delicious!

1. _leaves_   6. _____
2. _____   7. _____
3. _____   8. _____
4. _____   9. _____
5. _____   10. _____

Challenge Your class just attended an outdoor concert at the beach. Write a journal entry about your experience. Use three of the Challenge Words. Write on a separate sheet of paper.

Spelling Words

1. echoes
2. halves
3. solos
4. leaves
5. heroes
6. cliffs
7. scarves
8. potatoes
9. pianos
10. volcanoes
11. sheriffs
12. calves
13. tomatoes
14. cellos
15. wolves
16. ratios
17. stereos
18. yourselves
19. studios
20. bookshelves

Challenge
vetoes
mosquitoes
avocados
wharves
sopranos

**The Princess Who
Became a King**
Spelling: Plurals

Spelling Word Sort

Write each Basic Word beside the correct heading.

Add -s	
Add -es	
Change f to v and add -es	

Challenge Add the Challenge Words to your Word Sort.

Spelling Words

1. echoes
2. halves
3. solos
4. leaves
5. heroes
6. cliffs
7. scarves
8. potatoes
9. pianos
10. volcanoes
11. sheriffs
12. calves
13. tomatoes
14. cellos
15. wolves
16. ratios
17. stereos
18. yourselves
19. studios
20. bookshelves

Challenge
vetoes
mosquitoes
avocados
wharves
sopranos

Proofreading for Spelling

Find the misspelled words and circle them. Write them correctly on the lines below.

It's hard to imagine now, but in the late 1800s archaeologists were treated like movie stars are today. Digging in the sands of Egypt, the clifs of Asia, or beneath tropical volcanos, these popular heros traveled in comfort. Their tents were lined with bookshelfs. Famous scientists did not make their travels alone—soloes were not their style. They often took along their "better halfs" and a small army of assistants. Full studioes of artists and writers recorded their activities. At home, they were almost royalty. Dinner parties where women wore formal dresses and flowing scarfs were common. There were no stereoes at the time, so parties featured live musicians with pianoes, celloes, violins, and other instruments. Can you picture yourselfs being treated so grandly if you were archaeologists today?

Spelling Words

1. echoes
2. halves
3. solos
4. leaves
5. heroes
6. cliffs
7. scarves
8. potatoes
9. pianos
10. volcanoes
11. sheriffs
12. calves
13. tomatoes
14. cellos
15. wolves
16. ratios
17. stereos
18. yourselves
19. studios
20. bookshelves

1. _____ 7. _____
2. _____ 8. _____
3. _____ 9. _____
4. _____ 10. _____
5. _____ 11. _____
6. _____ 12. _____

Name _____ Date _____

Lesson 19
READER'S NOTEBOOK

The Princess Who
Became a King
Grammar: Punctuation

Correct Punctuation

An **appositive** is a word or group of words that follows a noun to identify or explain it. Depending on where the appositive appears in the sentence, it may be set off by one or two commas.

Thinking Questions
Which word or phrase tells more about a noun? Which noun does the word or phrase explain?

appositive at the end of a sentence

The archeologist Herbert E. Winlock made a discovery, <u>one that changed history</u>.

appositive in the middle of a sentence

He discovered that a woman, <u>Princess Hatshepsut</u>, had become a pharaoh!

Activity Underline the appositive. Use commas to correctly punctuate the appositive in each sentence.

1. A courageous woman, <u>Hatshepsut</u> reigned during Egypt's eighteenth dynasty.

2. Hatshepsut took good care of her subjects, <u>the people of Egypt</u>.

3. Her reign, <u>lasting 22 years</u> was successful.

4. All the rulers, <u>called pharaohs</u> before her were men.

5. She brought changes, <u>most importantly wealth and trade</u> to her people.

6. Her greatest project, <u>her burial temple</u> was built by her advisor Senenmut.

7. There is much to learn about Hatshepsut, <u>a brave and daring woman</u>.

Name _____ Date _____

Lesson 19
READER'S NOTEBOOK

**The Princess Who
Became a King**
Grammar: Punctuation

Commas and Parentheses

Commas set off a **nonrestrictive element** that makes sense as part of the main sentence.

Hatshepsut, unlike Egyptian royal women before her, ruled as a pharaoh.

Parentheses set off a **parenthetical element** that shows a break in thought.

She was a princess before she declared herself pharaoh (king of Egypt).

Thinking Questions
What information can be removed without changing the meaning of the sentence? Does it make sense as part of the main sentence? Does it show a break in thought?

Activity Underline the nonrestrictive or parenthetical element in each sentence. Place commas around a nonrestrictive element. Place parentheses around a parenthetical element.

1. Royal women (like royal men) played an important role in Egyptian religion.

2. Hatshepsut (upon her death) was mummified.

3. She was famous throughout the land (the kingdom of Egypt).

4. I read an interesting book, the topic was mummies .

5. I searched the sources, including the bibliography for information.

6. The author writes about her successful reign on page 2 (the book's introduction).

7. These books, which I returned are not historically accurate.

8. Professionals (scholars and archaeologists) debate the date of her death.

Name _____ Date _____

Dashes

Dashes are used to set off parenthetical elements that explain a word or phrase. Depending on where the parenthetical expression appears in the sentence, it may be set off by one or two dashes.

parenthetical element at the end of a sentence

I watched an interesting show—a documentary about King Tutankhamen.

parenthetical element in the middle of a sentence

King Tutankhamen—he is known as "the boy king"—was a young boy when he became a pharaoh.

> **Thinking Question**
> *Which part of the sentence shows a change in thought?*

Activity Determine whether each sentence contains a parenthetical element. If it does, rewrite the sentence to include dashes. Write *no dash* on the line if none is needed.

1. Our class went to the museum to see the Egyptian exhibit.

   Our class went to the museum—to see the Egyptian exhibit

2. The exhibit five rooms filled with artifacts was very large.

   _____

   _____

3. The pharaoh's thrones he had three in all were beautiful.

   _____

   _____

4. We saw the pharaoh's sandals in one of the rooms.

   _____

   _____

Subject-Verb Agreement

<u>Mattie</u> **has** a book about the pharaohs.
<u>We</u> **were searching** the shelves in the nonfiction section of the library.
<u>Lucy and Eric</u> **chose** books about mummies.
Either my <u>sister</u> or <u>Eric</u> **is taking** the photographs.
There **are** beautiful <u>photographs</u> of the pyramids in Eric's book.
Neither my <u>friends</u> nor <u>I</u> **have found** any books about King Tut.

1–5. **Underline the correct verb in parentheses to complete each sentence.**

1. My classmates and I (is, are) studying ancient Egypt.
2. One of the ancient Egyptian obelisks still (stand, stands) today.
3. Their design and construction (remain, remains) a marvel to historians.
4. Either Karen or Pedro (has, have) registered for the course.
5. Neither the students nor the teacher (know, knows) the answer.

6–10. **This note has five errors in subject-verb agreement. Use proofreading marks to correct the note.**

To: My party advisor

I am celebrating my thirtieth birthday. My husband, the prince, and I has

high expectations. People from all over the kingdom is coming for the party.

There are a lot to do before then. First, either you or your assistants has

the job of decorating the palace. The prince and I wants our palace to

look exceptionally beautiful.

Name _____ Date _____

Lesson 19
READER'S NOTEBOOK

The Princess Who
Became a King
Grammar: Connect to Writing

Connect to Writing

Good writers keep their writing interesting by writing longer sentences that include appositives and nonrestrictive and parenthetical elements.

appositives make writing clearer

I went to the library, the one by my house, to check out books on ancient Egypt.

nonrestrictive and parenthetical elements explain

The books, all of which are about the 18th dynasty, provide great information.

The archaeologists' photographs (from the 1920s) are fascinating.

The pyramids—burial chambers for the pharaohs—are mysterious.

1–3.   Add appositives to explain nouns more clearly.

1. We approached the sarcophagus.

_____

_____

2. The lecturer talked about ancient Egypt.

_____

_____

3. They used small shovels and brushes.

_____

_____

4–5.   Add nonrestrictive or parenthetical elements to explain information in each sentence.

4. The mummy was on the examination table.

_____

_____

5. We saw the pyramids on Saturday morning.

_____

Name _____ Date _____

Lesson 19
READER'S NOTEBOOK

The Princess Who
Became a King
Writing: Informative Writing

Focus Trait: Organization
Introductions

An introduction lets the reader know what your topic is and why it is important. It gives readers a glimpse of what they will be reading about in your report. A well-written introduction will have the reader wanting to read more.

The following sentences of an introductory paragraph are out of order. On the lines below, write the paragraph so that the sentences follow logical order.

One of the areas in which she succeeded was warfare.

She also gained much wealth for Egypt.

Hatshepsut was different from other female rulers of Egypt.

With that prosperity, she was able to initiate many building projects, which are examples of some of the greatest architecture in Egyptian history.

Yet even though she triumphed in war, Hatshepsut brought about a peaceful era.

Unlike these others, she reigned for a very long time and enjoyed great success.

_____

_____

_____

_____

_____

_____

_____

_____

_____

_____

 Reader's Guide

Bodies from the Ash: Life and Death in Ancient Pompeii

CREATE A DRAWING WITH LABELS AND CALLOUTS

The author of this text creates vivid images of Pompeii during the volcanic eruption and its excavation.

Use these descriptions to draw a picture of Pompeii at different times. Label your drawing with callout sentences to provide more details. Below your drawing, provide a summary of the text. Remember to base your summary on facts not your opinions.

Read pages 584–585. Then draw your illustration and write a summary.

AUGUST 24 79 C.E.

[drawing box]

SUMMARY:

_____

_____

Name _____ Date _____

Read the fourth, fifth, and sixth paragraphs on page 588.
Then draw your illustration and write a summary.

AUGUST 25 79 C.E.

SUMMARY:

_____

_____

Read the third and fourth paragraphs on page 591 and all of page 592.
Then draw your illustration and write a summary.

1700s

SUMMARY:

_____

_____

Prefixes *un-, re-, in-, im-, ir-, il-*

Bodies from the Ash
Vocabulary Strategies: Prefixes
un-, re-, in-, im-, ir-, il-

The words below all begin with a prefix. Choose a word from the box that best completes each sentence. Then give a definition for the word you chose.

> illogical   insufficient   irresistible
> reconnect   impolite   rediscover
> unexpected   incapable   impatient

1. The speaker's ideas were _____ and made no sense.

   _____

2. An _____ answer can end a conversation.

   _____

3. Without the facts, a detective is _____ of solving the

   mystery. _____

4. The electrician had to _____ the cable to the socket.

   _____

5. There was _____ light to continue playing outside.

   _____

6. The _____ gift made his grandparents smile.

   _____

7. It is fun to _____ old letters and photographs.

   _____

8. After waiting for half an hour, the bus driver felt _____.

   _____

9. Going for a swim on such a hot day was _____.

   _____

Prefixes: *dis-, ex-, inter-*

Basic Write the Basic Word that is the antonym of the word or group of words listed.

1. love _____

2. comply _____

3. agree to _____

4. satisfy _____

5. implosion _____

6. import _____

7. solidify _____

8. local _____

9. admiration _____

10. approve _____

11. put together _____

Challenge Imagine that you are an archaeologist who has discovered an unknown prehistoric animal. Write an article describing your find. Use three of the Challenge Words. Write on a separate sheet of paper.

Spelling Words

1. disobey
2. explosion
3. dislike
4. interview
5. disapprove
6. interoffice
7. Internet
8. disallow
9. disappear
10. international
11. disrespect
12. exchange
13. exclaim
14. dissolve
15. disconnect
16. interact
17. distaste
18. export
19. disappoint
20. interstate

Challenge
exterminate
interrupt
intermediate
intercept
disproportion

Spelling Word Sort

Write each Basic Word beside the correct heading.

dis-	
ex-	
inter-	

Challenge Add the Challenge Words to your Word Sort.

Spelling Words

1. disobey
2. explosion
3. dislike
4. interview
5. disapprove
6. interoffice
7. Internet
8. disallow
9. disappear
10. international
11. disrespect
12. exchange
13. exclaim
14. dissolve
15. disconnect
16. interact
17. distaste
18. export
19. disappoint
20. interstate

Challenge
exterminate
interrupt
intermediate
intercept
disproportion

Proofreading for Spelling

Find the misspelled words and circle them. Write them correctly on the lines below.

Abbie searched the Innernet all evening for information on archaeological digs. She did not want to desobey or direspekt her mother, but the dishes could wait. Only one day before, Abbie's deslike for science was bigger than her disstate for beets. After her intervue with famed archaeologist Dr. Janik, however, Abbie had changed her tune.

Abbie had listened intently to Dr. Janik discuss inernational digs that unraveled mysteries of the past. Dr. Janik also recalled the dangers of archaeological digs. "Sometimes, precious artifacts dissappear. Thieves eksport them over innerstate lines and sell them in exschange for large amounts of money."

"Abbie! Come do the dishes!" she heard her mom eksclaim. Abbie ran into the kitchen to tell her mom about her new dream—to become an archaeologist.

Spelling Words
1. disobey
2. explosion
3. dislike
4. interview
5. disapprove
6. interoffice
7. Internet
8. disallow
9. disappear
10. international
11. disrespect
12. exchange
13. exclaim
14. dissolve
15. disconnect
16. interact
17. distaste
18. export
19. disappoint
20. interstate

1. _____   7. _____

2. _____   8. _____

3. _____   9. _____

4. _____   10. _____

5. _____   11. _____

6. _____   12. _____

Name _____ Date _____

Lesson 20
READER'S NOTEBOOK

Bodies from the Ash
Grammar: Prepositions;
Prepositional Phrases

Prepositions and Prepositional Phrases

A **preposition** links nouns and pronouns to other words in a sentence. The noun or pronoun that comes after a preposition is its object. Some prepositions are: *on, about, beneath, beside, during,* and *across*.

A **prepositional phrase** is made up of a preposition, its object, and any words modifying the object.

preposition
We discovered many artifacts during the dig.

prepositional phrase
The ancient coins are in the museum.

Thinking Questions
Does the word link a noun or pronoun to other words in the sentence? Is it followed by an object and modifying words?

Activity Underline the prepositional phrase in each sentence. Circle the prepositions.

1. The city of Pompeii was buried.
2. The archaeologist dug a hole with special tools.
3. People gathered around the archaeologists.
4. They found pieces of animal bone.
5. Objects from daily life were unearthed.
6. They found lava bedrock below the city.
7. Pompeii is not far from Vesuvius.
8. Many earthquakes occurred in the area.

Name _____ Date _____

Adjective and Adverb Phrases

A prepositional phrase may be used as an adjective to modify a noun or pronoun. An **adjective phrase** tells *which one* or *what kind*. A **prepositional phrase** may be used as an adverb to modify a verb, adjective, or adverb. An **adverb phrase** tells *how, when, where, how much,* or *why*.

> **Thinking Questions**
> *Does the word tell more about a noun or pronoun? Or does it tell more about a verb, adjective, or adverb?*

     noun   **prepositional phrase as adjective**
On Monday <u>of next week</u> we go to the museum.

       verb   **prepositional phrase as adverb**
We will learn a lot <u>about Pompeii and Vesuvius</u>.

Activity In each sentence, underline the prepositional phrase. Circle the word that it modifies and write the type of phrase it is on the line.

1. We arrived at the museum early. _____

2. The boy with the red hair asked a question. _____

3. Pompeii thrived for many years. _____

4. Ships from many countries used Pompeii's port. _____

5. Pompeii was a place for vacation. _____

6. In ten minutes we will leave the museum. _____

Prepositional Phrases: Punctuation

If a **prepositional phrase** begins a sentence and is made up of four or more words, it should be followed by a comma. If a prepositional phrase is part of the main clause, no comma is needed.

prepositional phrase with comma

Before the August eruption, people thought Vesuvius was extinct.

prepositional phrases without comma

Ancient people didn't recognize the earthquakes as serious volcano warnings.

In modern times we know the warning signs better.

Thinking Questions
Does the prepositional phrase begin the sentence? Is it made up of four words or more?

Activity Place a comma after the prepositional phrase in the sentence when needed. Write *no comma* on the line if none is needed.

1. Many towns were located at Mount Vesuvius' base. _____

2. Super-hot ash and gases rushed toward them. _____

3. Throughout the busy town people were startled. _____

4. People ran for their lives when they saw the danger. _____

5. Inside their villas and houses people hid under furniture. _____

6. Bodies were found under thick layers of ash and rocks. _____

7. Across the formerly fertile valley farms were buried. _____

8. After centuries people forgot the towns had ever been there. _____

Perfect Tenses

Present perfect tense	I **have studied** science for three years.
Past perfect tense	You **had studied** science before last year's class.
Future perfect tense	By the end of the year, you **will have studied** science more than anyone else in our class.

1–4. Write the correct form of *have* for the tense shown in parentheses.

1. People _____ worried about natural disasters for centuries. (present perfect)

2. Today, scientists _____ discovered new ways to predict natural disasters. (present perfect)

3. Centuries ago most people _____ learned little about volcanoes. (past perfect)

4. Who knows what scientists _____ learned about volcanoes in another hundred years? (future perfect)

5–8. Correct the tense of each underlined verb.

5. Terrance <u>have learned</u> about volcanoes last year. _____

6. By next month we <u>have learned</u> all about earthquakes. _____

7. By noon yesterday Jason <u>have finished</u> his science project. _____

8. Melinda <u>have studied</u> volcanoes for the past three months. _____

Connect to Writing

Two sentences can be combined by using a **prepositional phrase**.
separate sentences I checked out three books today. They were about natural disasters.
combined sentence I checked out three books about natural disasters today.

Combine each of the sentence pairs into one sentence using a prepositional phrase. Write the new sentence on the line.

1. We approached the active volcano. We approached it with care.

   _____

2. The lecturer talked about Pompeii. She talked in a very loud voice.

   _____

3. Alcubierre searched for Pompeii. He looked near an unfinished underground canal.

   _____

4. They found the first skeleton and some coins. This happened after twenty days.

   _____

5. The hoard of coins was a great treasure. It was next to the rich man.

   _____

6. I would like to see the treasures of Pompeii. I'll do it after high school.

   _____

7. It would be more fun to go with someone. I'd choose my older sister.

   _____

8. My sister likes to study maps. She finds them in travel books.

   _____

Focus Trait: Evidence
Paraphrasing

Good writers paraphrase by putting an author's words into their own words.

Author's Words	Paraphrase
Over the course of two days, Mount Vesuvius erupted, causing destruction in the city of Pompeii.	The city of Pompeii experienced two harrowing days of Mount Vesuvius's eruption.

Paraphrase each of the following sentences, using your own words.

1. Mount Vesuvius was considered to be a sacred mountain to the god Hercules, according to the Romans.

   _____

   _____

2. Hercules, one of Jupiter's sons, was known in Roman mythology for his extraordinary strength.

   _____

   _____

3. A powerful military presence, the city-state of Sparta was in control of much of ancient Greece.

   _____

   _____

4. Among its well-known works of art, Athens boasts the Parthenon and many great monuments.

   _____

   _____

Name _____ Date _____

Unit 4
READER'S NOTEBOOK

A Wrinkle in Time
Segment 1
Independent Reading

A Wrinkle in Time

Wanted!

On pages 17–23, the author introduces us to Mrs. Whatsit. Use textual evidence to answer these questions about Mrs. Whatsit.

What is her age?

_____

_____

What is she wearing?

_____

_____

What does she sound like?

_____

_____

What does she look like?

_____

_____

Name _____ Date _____

We find out from Charles Wallace that Mrs. Whatsit stole the sheets from Mrs. Buncombe. Use your answers to the questions and the text on pages 5–23 to create a wanted poster describing the crime and giving details about the suspect.

WANTED

Have you seen this person?

Wanted for:

_____

Description:

_____

_____

_____

Witnesses say:

_____

_____

_____

Name _____ Date _____

Unit 4
READER'S NOTEBOOK

A Wrinkle in Time
Segment 1
Independent Reading

Write Journal Entries

On pages 24–38, the author gives us more information about Meg and Charles Wallace and introduces us to Calvin. What happens to these characters on this day? Describe each character's day in his or her own words. Focus on the events and how the characters react to them.

Dear Diary,

_____

_____

_____

_____

_____

_____

_____

_____

Meg

Name _____ Date _____

Unit 4
READER'S NOTEBOOK

A Wrinkle in Time
Segment 1
Independent Reading

Dear Diary,

_____

_____

_____

_____

_____

_____

Calvin

Dear Diary,

_____

_____

_____

_____

_____

_____

Charles Wallace

Name _____ Date _____

Unit 4
READER'S NOTEBOOK

A Wrinkle in Time
Segment 2
Independent Reading

Reader's Guide

A Wrinkle in Time

Missing!

We learn in the first chapters that Meg and Charles Wallace's father is missing. What has happened to him? Use textual evidence from pages 39–54 to help you understand more about this "missing person's case."

What rumor do people believe about Meg's father?

_____

_____

What is his profession?

_____

With whom does he work?

_____

Where did he live?

_____

_____

When was the last contact Meg and Charles and their mother had with their father?

_____

_____

Name _____ Date _____

Meg is convinced that her father is alive and simply missing. Use your notes to help her make a missing person's ad to help her find him.

★ NEWS TODAY ★

MISSING!!

Who: Dr. Murry

Occupation: _____

Last seen: _____

Last known activity: _____

_____

Last contact: _____

_____

Other information! _____

_____

_____

_____

_____

_____

Vote Today

Dog Saves Child

Name _____ Date _____

Unit 4
READER'S NOTEBOOK

A Wrinkle in Time
Segment 2
Independent Reading

Write Postcards to Mother

As the children begin their journey, what happens to them? How do
they feel about it? Suppose Meg writes postcards to her mother.
Write about their experiences in Meg's words.

Dear Mother,

_____

_____

_____

_____

_____

_____

_____

_____

_____

Love,
Meg

Mrs. Murry
United States
Planet Earth

32¢

Name _____ Date _____

Unit 4
READER'S NOTEBOOK

A Wrinkle in Time
Segment 2
Independent Reading

Use the text starting on page 66 to describe where
the children visited. Write this description in another
postcard from Meg to her mother. Remember to write
the postcard from Meg's point of view.

Dear Mother,

_____

_____

_____

_____

_____

_____

_____

_____

_____

Love,
Meg

Mrs. Murry
United States
Planet Earth

32¢

Name _____ Date _____

Unit 4
READER'S NOTEBOOK

A Wrinkle in Time
Segment 2
Independent Reading

Prepare a Slide Show Presentation

The children learn about the tessaract. Suppose you were asked to prepare an exciting slide show presentation explaining how space travel may be possible. Use words and pictures to answer the heading question on each slide. Use the text on pages 72–79 to help you.

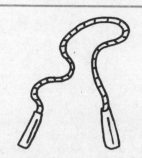

Why Is a Tessaract Necessary?

Name _____ Date _____

Unit 4
READER'S NOTEBOOK

A Wrinkle in Time
Segment 2
Independent Reading

What Is It Like to Travel by Tessaract?

What Are Some of the Dangers of Traveling by Tessaract?

Name _____ Date _____

Unit 4
READER'S NOTEBOOK

A Wrinkle in Time
Segment 3
Independent Reading

A Wrinkle in Time

Draw a Picture

Meg, Charles Wallace, and Calvin meet the Happy Medium.
She shows them a view of Earth. Then, they learn more about
Mrs. Whatsit. Use textual details from pages 87–93 to draw a
picture of what they see. Then write a short description.

_____

_____

Interview with the Happy Medium

Imagine that an interviewer wants to find out more about the Happy Medium's role in helping the children. Use the text on pages 87–93 to help the Happy Medium answer the interview questions.

Why did you ask the children if they wanted to see their mothers?

_____

_____

_____

Why did you feel badly afterwards?

_____

_____

_____

What will you do now?

_____

_____

_____

Name _____ Date _____

Unit 4
READER'S NOTEBOOK

A Wrinkle in Time
Segment 3
Independent Reading

Compare and Contrast

On pages 99–108, the children enter Camazotz. Think about how Camazotz might compare with your city. Mark each trait below as the same or different. Then provide support from the text for your answer.

Trait	Same	Different	Textual Evidence
the type of houses			_____ _____ _____ _____
the way the children play			_____ _____ _____ _____ _____
the types of buildings			_____ _____ _____ _____
types of jobs			_____ _____ _____ _____ _____
order and organization			_____ _____ _____ _____

Name _____ Date _____

Unit 4
READER'S NOTEBOOK

A Wrinkle in Time
Segment 3
Independent Reading

Make a Travel Guide to Camazotz

Use the chart you completed and the text to create a travel guide to Camazotz telling people what it looks like and what to expect. In the empty box, draw a picture that will help travelers know what to expect.

Travel to Camazotz!

What will you see?

_____
_____
_____
_____
_____
_____
_____
_____

What can you do?

_____
_____
_____
_____
_____
_____

Camazotz is the perfect place for YOU if . . .

_____
_____
_____
_____
_____
_____

Name _____ Date _____

Unit 4
READER'S NOTEBOOK

A Wrinkle in Time
Segment 4
Independent Reading

 Reader's Guide

A Wrinkle in Time

Make a List

On pages 127–137, Charles Wallace comes under the influence of IT. Use evidence from the text to help Meg make a list of the signs that someone is controlled by the IT. Write each sign in the form of a *yes/no* question.

Is Someone You Love Controlled by IT?

- _____
  _____

- _____
  _____

- _____
  _____

- _____
  _____

- _____
  _____

- _____
  _____

Name _____ Date _____

Unit 4
READER'S NOTEBOOK

A Wrinkle in Time
Segment 4
Independent Reading

Write a Letter

Take a look at your checklist and consider the details on pages 127–137 of the text. What would Charles Wallace want to tell Meg at this point in the story? As Charles Wallace, write an e-mail to Meg. Be sure to use his point of view!

New Message

From: **Charles Wallace**

To: **Meg**

Subject: **The IT**

_____

_____

_____

_____

_____

_____

_____

Name _____ Date _____

Make a Timeline

Meg, Calvin, and Charles Wallace finally find Dr. Murry.
Use the events on pages 138–156 to create a timeline of
the events in this chapter. Remember to place the events
on the timeline in the order in which they happened.

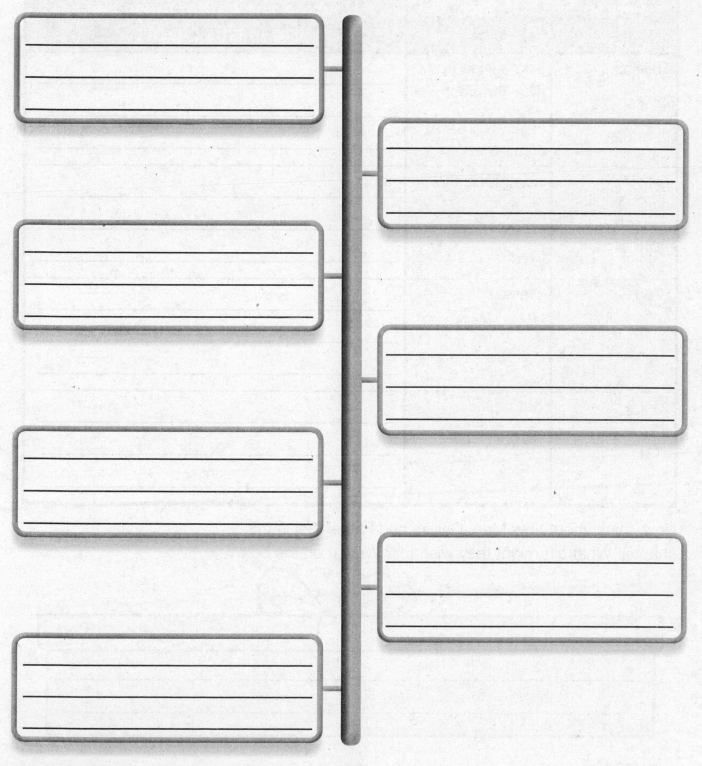

Name _____ Date _____

Unit 4
READER'S NOTEBOOK

A Wrinkle in Time
Segment 4
Independent Reading

Giving Gifts

When they arrive in Camazotz, the children receive gifts.
Use your timeline to recall the gifts in the chapter. Think
about how the children use their gifts.

Person	Gift	How did the children use their gifts in this chapter?
Calvin	some lines from *The Tempest*	_____ _____ _____
Calvin	communication	_____ _____ _____
Meg	glasses	_____ _____ _____
Meg	her faults	_____ _____ _____

Now, think about how Meg, Calvin, and Father feel in this
chapter. What gift might they wish for? Write it on the box.

_____

_____

Name _____ Date _____

Unit 4
READER'S NOTEBOOK

A Wrinkle in Time
Segment 4
Independent Reading

Notes from Father's Experience

As they are waiting for Meg to feel better, Father shares some of his experience. Use textual evidence to help you answer the questions.

Use page 158.
How does Father explain how they were able to withstand IT for so long?

_____

_____

_____

Use page 158. How does IT operate?

_____

_____

_____

Use pages 158–159. Why does IT get to Charles Wallace and not Meg and Calvin?

_____

_____

_____

Use page 164. For what reason does Father tesser?

_____

_____

_____

Use page 164. Why does Father say they left Charles Wallace behind?

_____

_____

_____

Name _____ Date _____

Unit 4
READER'S NOTEBOOK

A Wrinkle in Time
Segment 4
Independent Reading

Make a Book Cover and a Table of Contents

Suppose Father, Calvin, and Meg wrote a book about how to escape Camazotz. Think about Father's notes on the previous page and details from the text. Design an engaging cover and think of a good title. Then write a table of contents that includes at least five chapters.

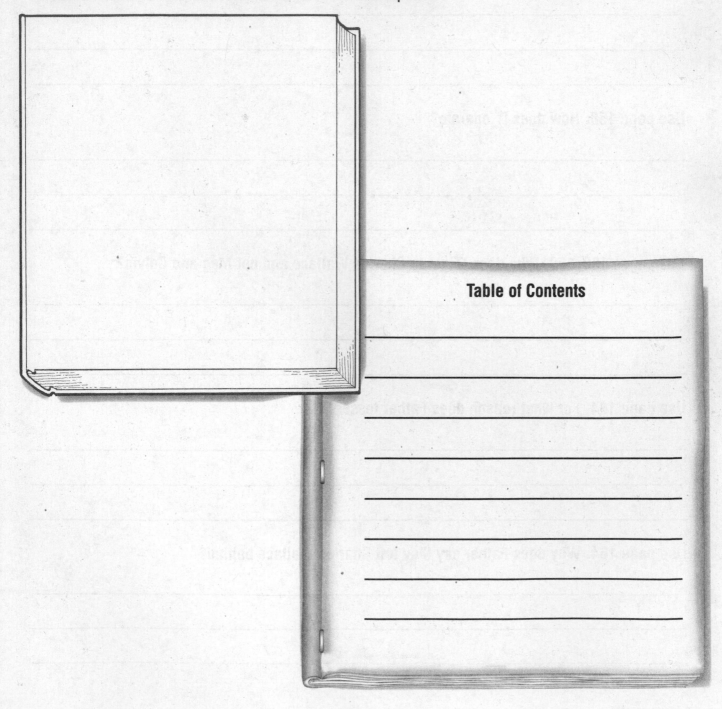

Table of Contents

Name _____ Date _____

Unit 4
READER'S NOTEBOOK

A Wrinkle in Time
Segment 5
Independent Reading

Reader's Guide

A Wrinkle in Time

Draw and Label a Picture

Suppose you were a scientist traveling with Meg, Calvin, and Father and just discovered the creatures on the new planet. Use the text on pages 169–175 to understand these creatures. Then draw and label a picture to describe them.

Name _____ Date _____

Unit 4
READER'S NOTEBOOK

A Wrinkle in Time
Segment 5
Independent Reading

The Aunt Beast Award

In Chapter 11, Meg is healed by the creature that she names *"Aunt Beast."* Meg would like to present Aunt Beast with an award for her help. Write Meg's speech that she would use when presenting Aunt Beast with her award.

_____

_____

_____

_____

_____

_____

_____

_____

_____

_____

_____

Name _____ Date _____

Unit 4
READER'S NOTEBOOK

A Wrinkle in Time
Segment 5
Independent Reading

Interviews with the Characters

Suppose you had the chance to interview some of
the characters in the book. Use the text from pages 169–202
to help you answer the questions. Answer the questions from
the points of view of Meg, Calvin, and Father.

INTERVIEW WITH MEG

You were afraid to go back to Camazotz. What convinced you to go?

_____

_____

_____

How did you rescue him?

_____

_____

_____

Do you think you learned anything on this journey?

_____

_____

_____

Name _____ Date _____

Unit 4
READER'S NOTEBOOK

A Wrinkle in Time
Segment 5
Independent Reading

INTERVIEW WITH CALVIN

What did you have to say to Mrs. Whatsit when you met again?

_____

_____

What did Mrs. Whatsit say to help you understand the difference between Earth and Camazotz?

_____

_____

What do you think Mrs. Whatsit meant by her sonnet analogy?

_____

_____

INTERVIEW WITH FATHER

Why didn't you want Mrs. Whatsit to take Meg back?

_____

_____

How did you feel about Mrs. Whatsit and Mrs. Who? Why?

_____

_____

How did you feel to see Meg again?

_____

_____

Name _____ Date _____

Lesson 21
READER'S NOTEBOOK

All Alone in the
Universe
Independent Reading

All Alone in the Universe

Write an Advice Column

In this story, Debbie struggles when her best friend
Maureen makes a new friend. Suppose that Debbie
is writing a friendship advice column for her school news
paper. Use examples from the text to help Debbie respond
to the writer's questions.

Read pages 616–617. Then write a response from Debbie's point of view.

Dear Debbie,

My best friend and I always go to the carnival together. This year, I want to invite a
new friend I made at camp to come with us. Do you think this is a good idea?

Curious Camper

Dear Curious Camper,

_____

_____

_____

_____

Best Wishes,
Debbie

Read page 619. Then write a response from Debbie's point of view.

Dear Debbie,

Lately I have been hanging out with a girl from my soccer team. I always invite my best friend, but she is so quiet when she is with us. I am not sure what's going on. Any ideas?

Soccer Star

Dear Soccer Star,

_____

_____

_____

_____

_____

_____

Best Wishes,

Debbie

Word Relationships

Determine the word relationship for each word pair below.
Then write the word pairs in the correct column in the chart.

carrot/vegetable bird/flock birthday/celebration blackout/darkness folktale/story
flour/bread greyhound/dog gymnast/athlete hammer/tool hurricane/damage
leg/body member/group plateau/landform read/learn shirt/clothing
success/happiness singer/choir steering wheel/car thirsty/drink thread/cloth

Cause/Effect	Part/Whole	Item/Category

Name _____ Date _____

Prefixes: *pre-, pro-*

Basic Write the Basic Word that best completes each group.

1. safeguard, care, _____

2. announce, shout, _____

3. stop, avoid, _____

4. put off, make longer, _____

5. stick out, jut, _____

6. old, ancient, _____

7. demand, condition, _____

8. win, succeed, _____

9. assume, jump to conclusions, _____

10. method, technique, _____

Challenge Write an editorial for the school paper comparing candidates for class president. Be sure to include several of your opinions. Use three of the Challenge Words. Write on a separate sheet of paper.

Spelling Words

1. prediction
2. project
3. prevent
4. prepaid
5. prevail
6. proclaim
7. prehistoric
8. prejudge
9. preapprove
10. pregame
11. precaution
12. preorder
13. prescreen
14. preshow
15. pretreat
16. prolong
17. process
18. protrude
19. provision
20. production

Challenge
prologue
proportion
prorate
preseason
prearrange

Spelling Word Sort

All Alone in the Universe
Spelling: Prefixes: *pre-, pro-*

Write each Basic Word beside the correct heading.

Prefix *pre-*	
Prefix *pro-*	

Challenge   Add the Challenge Words to your Word Sort.

Spelling Words

1. prediction
2. project
3. prevent
4. prepaid
5. prevail
6. proclaim
7. prehistoric
8. prejudge
9. preapprove
10. pregame
11. precaution
12. preorder
13. prescreen
14. preshow
15. pretreat
16. prolong
17. process
18. protrude
19. provision
20. production

Challenge
prologue
proportion
prorate
preseason
prearrange

Proofreading for Spelling

Find the misspelled words and circle them. Write them correctly on the lines below.

Rajanha watched her mother pretreet her little sister with sunscreen. "Your hat won't preject enough shadow on your face. Be still!" Her mother took procautin when it came to the sun. "You'll thank me when you're older and your skin doesn't look like a prehistorik dinosaur!"

Rajanha sighed. She wasn't going to the pool. She wasn't doing anything. Rajanha had preepayed for tickets to her school's progame dance. Her mother said she could go under the prevision that Rajanha did all of her chores, but her mom was skeptical. Her mother's predikshun had been right. In the prosess of planning, Rajanha had neglected them all.

Suddenly, there was a knock on the door. "Why do you want to porlong everything?!" Rajanha's best friend, Sara, asked when Rajanha answered the door. "Let me help you finish these chores and get you to the dance!"

"You're the best friend ever!" said Rajanha.

Spelling Words

1. prediction
2. project
3. prevent
4. prepaid
5. prevail
6. proclaim
7. prehistoric
8. prejudge
9. preapprove
10. pregame
11. precaution
12. preorder
13. prescreen
14. preshow
15. pretreat
16. prolong
17. process
18. protrude
19. provision
20. production

1. _____ 6. _____

2. _____ 7. _____

3. _____ 8. _____

4. _____ 9. _____

5. _____ 10. _____

Present Progressive Forms

The **present progressive** tense is used to talk about an action that is happening right now. To form the present progressive tense, add the present tense of *be* before a verb ending in *-ing*. The **present perfect progressive** tense describes an action that began in the past, continues now, and may continue in the future. It is formed by adding *has been* or *have been* before an *-ing* verb.

Thinking Questions
Does the sentence describe action that is continuing right now? Or does it describe action that began in the past, continues now, and may continue in the future?

> **present progressive**
>
> Maureen is <u>gazing</u> at the water.

> **present perfect progressive**
>
> She and I <u>have been coming</u> here for years

Activity Rewrite each sentence by changing the underlined verb to the verb tense in parentheses.

1. I <u>talk</u> to Glenna right now. (present progressive)

   _____

2. We <u>go</u> to the movies together. (present perfect progressive)

   _____

3. Glenna <u>tries</u> to be nice to you. (present progressive)

   _____

4. She <u>includes</u> you when we do things. (present perfect progressive)

   _____

5. She <u>hopes</u> I won't show up. (present perfect progressive)

   _____

6. You do not <u>try</u> very hard to understand her. (present progressive)

   _____

Past Progressive Forms

The **past progressive** tense is used to talk about a past action that happened at the same time as another action, or was in progress at some time in the past. It is formed by adding the past tense of *be* before a verb ending in *-ing*. The **past perfect progressive** tense describes a past, ongoing action that was completed before another past action. It is formed by adding *had been* before an *-ing* verb.

Thinking Questions
Does the verb describe past action that happened at the same time as another action or was in progress in the past? Or does it describe past, ongoing action that was completed before another past action?

past progressive
Dad <u>was cooking</u> dinner when the phone rang.

past perfect progressive
I <u>had been doing</u> chores before Maureen called.

Activity Rewrite each sentence by changing the underlined verb to the verb tense in parentheses.

1. Maureen said she <u>read</u> about a movie. (past perfect progressive)

_____

2. She <u>wondered</u> if I wanted to see it with her. (past progressive).

_____

3. I said I <u>planned</u> to see the movie tonight, too. (past progressive)

_____

4. The weatherperson <u>predicted</u> rain. (past perfect progressive)

_____

5. We <u>walked</u> for two minutes before the rain started. (past perfect progressive)

_____

6. We <u>dripped</u> by the time we got to the theater. (past progressive)

_____

Name _____ Date _____

Future Progressive Forms

The **future progressive tense** is used to talk about an action that will happen at some time in the future. To form the future progressive tense, add *will be* before a verb ending in *-ing*. The **future perfect progressive tense** describes an ongoing action that will be completed at a specific future time. It is formed by adding *will have been* before an *-ing* verb.

Thinking Questions
Does the verb describe an action that will happen in the future? Or does it describe an ongoing action that will be completed at a certain time in the future?

future progressive
The Flaibers <u>will be leaving</u> Saturday morning.

future perfect progressive
They <u>will have been packing</u> their bags for days.

Activity Rewrite each sentence by changing the underlined verb to the verb tense in parentheses.

1. Maureen <u>goes</u> with them to Borth Lake. (future progressive)

   _____

2. She and Glenna <u>talk</u> about this for weeks. (future perfect progressive)

   _____

3. Maureen <u>sleeps</u> over at Glenna's house the night before. (future progressive)

   _____

4. They <u>travel</u> by car to Borth Lake. (future progressive)

   _____

5. Mr. Flaiber <u>prepares</u> the boat all day. (future perfect progressive)

   _____

6. They will <u>spend</u> lots of time in or on the water. (future progressive)

   _____

Correct Pronouns

Subject pronouns	**We** will enjoy the rides at the carnival. **It** will be lots of fun.
Object pronouns	Maureen asked me to go on **them** with **her**.
Demonstrative pronouns	**This** is the first year she will go on **that** ride alone.
Indefinite pronouns	**All** of us want to see **someone** dressed as a clown.
Intensive pronouns	I have never had any fear of clowns **myself**.

1–6. **Look at the underlined pronoun in each sentence. Write the type of pronoun it is on the line.**

1. Everyone in town is going to the carnival. _____

2. That is where we'll go on rides and play games. _____

3. My brother wants to win a game himself. _____

4. I am trying to win a baseball cap for him, too. _____

5. He doesn't know yet what I am doing. _____

6. I love surprising someone with a gift. _____

7–8. **Replace any unclear pronouns. Write the new sentence on the line.**

7. The pirate ship ride is exciting because of how far they swings back and forth.

_____

_____

8. I won a teddy bear and a plastic ring, but you don't know what to do with it.

_____

_____

Connect to Writing

Incorrect Verb Tenses	As we are walking by the river, she is smiling. I asked her what she has smiled about.
Correct Verb Tenses	As we were walking by the river, she was smiling. I asked her what she was smiling about.

Correct the underlined verb phrases. Write the new sentence on the line.

1. I was laughing and going on the rides, but I'm not enjoying myself.

_____

_____

2. They will be going on vacation together, and I was staying at home.

_____

_____

3. I've known Maureen for eight years, but I'm only knowing Glenna for six weeks.

_____

_____

4. I'm going to the river. Were you coming with me?

_____

_____

5. I have been trying to save money, but instead I had spent it.

_____

_____

6. I'm pleased to see that Maureen was getting out of the car.

_____

_____

Focus Trait: Elaboration
Showing Instead of Telling

Tells an Emotion	Shows the Emotion
I felt lousy.	My head was like a nail that had just been hammered into a wall.

Rewrite each sentence to show the emotion.

Tells an Emotion	Shows the Emotion
He felt excited.	
We were very sad.	
I felt nervous.	
They were extremely happy.	
She was anxious.	

Reader's Guide

First to Fly: How Wilbur & Orville Wright Invented the Airplane

Make a Timeline

The text in "First to Fly" is structured in sequential order. Read the text passages indicated in each part of the timeline. Complete the timeline of key events leading up to the first manned and powered flight.

Spring-Fall 1900

Summarize the events on page 644–645.

_____
_____
_____

July 1901

Summarize the events in the fourth paragraph of page 646.

_____
_____
_____

August 9, 1901

Summarize the events in the third paragraph of page 647.

_____
_____
_____

1902 | Summarize the events on page 648.
_____
_____
_____

1902 | Summarize the events on page 649.
_____
_____
_____

December 14, 1903 | Summarize the events in the third paragraph of page 651.
_____
_____
_____

December 17, 1903 | Summarize the caption on page 652.
_____
_____
_____

Based on the information you gathered, what conclusions can you draw about the process leading up to the first manned and powered flight?

_____
_____
_____

Denotation and Connotation

Choose a word from the box to complete each sentence. Then
circle + or − to show whether the word has a positive or negative
connotation, or feeling.

cheap	smile	antique	smirked
inexpensive	home	shack	outdated

1. You are welcome to visit my _____ any time.

+   −

2. The toy was _____ and didn't last long.

+   −

3. That _____ rug looks shabby next to the new furniture.

+   −

4. Peter _____ after he tricked his brother.

+   −

5. Jenny had a huge _____ on her face when she heard

that her best friend had won the contest.

+   −

6. I bought an _____ gift for my sister.

+   −

7. That _____ near the woods is not safe to enter.

+   −

8. My grandmother is very protective of her _____ dishes.

+   −

First to Fly
Spelling: Words with Silent Letters

Words with Silent Letters

Basic Write the Basic Word that best fits each clue.

1. do this before entering _____

2. to chew _____

3. fall _____

4. red fruit _____

5. information _____

6. a weapon _____

7. little pieces _____

8. unable to feel _____

9. land surrounded by water _____

10. a plan, or to plan _____

11. an amount owed _____

Challenge You are raising money for a local disaster relief fund. Write a letter to the editor of your local newspaper or website explaining the cause. Use three Challenge Words. Write on a separate sheet of paper.

Spelling Words

1. aisle
2. align
3. island
4. crumbs
5. gnaw
6. design
7. knotty
8. bustle
9. shepherd
10. soften
11. sword
12. thistle
13. knock
14. wrestle
15. column
16. autumn
17. knowledge
18. debt
19. numb
20. raspberry

Challenge
campaign
coup
solemn
yacht
pneumonia

Spelling Word Sort

Write each Basic Word beside the correct heading.

Silent letter at the beginning of the word	
Silent letter in the middle of the word	
Silent letter at the end of a word	

Challenge   Add the Challenge Words to your Word Sort.

Spelling Words

1. aisle
2. align
3. island
4. crumbs
5. gnaw
6. design
7. knotty
8. bustle
9. shepherd
10. soften
11. sword
12. thistle
13. knock
14. wrestle
15. column
16. autumn
17. knowledge
18. debt
19. numb
20. raspberry

Challenge
campaign
coup
solemn
yacht
pneumonia

Proofreading for Spelling

Find the misspelled words and circle them. Write them correctly on the lines below.

Kip woke up on an awtum day to a place he did not recognize. He looked around and realized that he was on an islund. A gust of wind blew through his notty hair, and his skin fclt knumb. To his nowlege, he had last been on a plane ride with Uncle Tom. He remembered feeling the plane drop and rushing down its aile to the cockpit. The plane was an old desine, but Uncle Tom would surely be able to handle any problems.

When Kip had seen his uncle wressle with the controls, his face as red as a razberry, Kip knew that there was trouble. "We're going down, Kip! I'll try to soffen the impact if I can!" The last thing Kip remembered was hearing the sound a giant might make if he tried to nok over a mountain.

Kip reached into his pocket, but all he found were crums. Then he realized that he had to find his uncle. He ran off into a patch of thisle calling for Uncle Tom.

Spelling Words

1. aisle
2. align
3. island
4. crumbs
5. gnaw
6. design
7. knotty
8. bustle
9. shepherd
10. soften
11. sword
12. thistle
13. knock
14. wrestle
15. column
16. autumn
17. knowledge
18. debt
19. numb
20. raspberry

1. _____   8. _____
2. _____   9. _____
3. _____   10. _____
4. _____   11. _____
5. _____   12. _____
6. _____   13. _____
7. _____

Direct Quotations

A **direct quotation** shows the exact words that someone says. Direct quotations are set off by quotation marks.

"I want to go to the park," I said.
Lance said, "You are my best friend."

Thinking Question
Which words tell exactly what the speaker is saying?

Activity Add quotation marks to the following sentences.

1. We have a lot of studying to do, said Liz.
2. Let's plan to fly down in March, said Miron.
3. We can go to the water park, I suggested.
4. I think that's a great idea, replied Kate.
5. She said, There is a water slide that is ten stories high.
6. I shouted, That sounds scary, but fun!
7. You can go if you get an *A* in science, my mom said.
8. I am so excited to fly on a plane, I said.

Name _____ Date _____

Lesson 22
READER'S NOTEBOOK

First to Fly
Grammar: Punctuation and
Quotations

Using Commas and Dashes

A **nonrestrictive element** is a piece of information that is non-essential to the basic meaning of the sentence. Set nonrestrictive elements off from the rest of the sentence with commas. A **parenthetical element** is a word or phrase that gives more information about part of the sentence. Use parentheses or dashes to set it off from the sentence.

Thinking Questions
Is the word or phrase non-essential to the meaning of the sentence? Does it give more information about part of the sentence?

nonrestrictive element

Waiting one more day, a rainy Tuesday, made all the difference.

parenthetical elements

Wilbur's final flight in 1903 was 852 feet (260 meters).

The brothers were in their 30s—Wilbur was 36 and Orville was 32—when they made their historic flight.

Activity Rewrite each sentence, setting off the additional information with commas, dashes, or parentheses.

1. The motor their custom-built engine was what made the Wright brothers' flight historic.

   _____

   _____

2. They continued to improve their airplane and set flight-time records 2 hours 19 minutes by 1908.

   _____

   _____

3. The brothers put on many demonstrations in France the 1908 record was set there.

   _____

   _____

Writing Dialogue

Dialogue is the written conversation between characters in a story. Use quotation marks around a character's exact words. Specify who is speaking and how. Use a comma to set off expressions like *she said* from the quotation itself. When a speaker changes, start a new paragraph. Use commas, dashes, and parentheses to set off nonrestrictive and parenthetical elements.

    Two friends, Marc and Kim, walked through the park. "I want a dog," he said. A lady walking her dog passed by quickly.

    "Dogs are difficult—a lot of responsibility," Kim suggested.

    "I know," he said sadly. "Maybe I'll get a cat."

Thinking Questions
How are quotation marks used in dialogue? How are commas, dashes, and parentheses used to show a speaker's meaning?

Activity Read each sentence. Then write a reply using dialogue.

1. "Where are we going?" asked Leighann.

_____

2. Brooks turned to Audree and said, "Let's listen to this new song."

_____

3. "Have you seen the new aviation exhibit at the museum?" asked Charlie.

_____

4. "How long is it running?" asked Charlie.

_____

5. "Can you pick up some bananas at the store?" asked Richard.

_____

6. "Are you going to the park?" asked Andre with a hopeful look in his eye.

_____

More Correct Pronouns

Intensive/Reflexive Pronouns	myself, yourself, himself, herself, itself, ourselves, yourselves, themselves
Intensive Pronoun	I want to learn to fly a plane **myself**.
Reflexive Pronoun	Will you please keep this news to **yourself** for now?

1–6. Look for the pronoun that ends in *-self* or *-selves.* Write whether it is *intensive* or *reflexive* on the line.

1. Martin wants to see for himself what flying is like. _____

2. We all must prove oursevles if we want to take lessons. _____

3. I myself need to keep my room cleaner. _____

4. How will you prove you can do it yourself? _____

5. A pilot is responsible for herself and all the other passengers. _____

6. The plane itself is just a tool. _____

7–9. Rewrite each sentence to fix the vague pronoun.

7. Michael, will you tell her that I have it?

_____

8. They must show they are ready to do this.

_____

9. We went there and met them.

_____

Connect to Writing

Dialogue Written Incorrectly	I've never flown before Cindy said. "It's not bad, said Lisa. It makes traveling faster".
Dialogue Written Correctly	"I've never flown before," Cindy said. "It's not bad," said Lisa. "It makes traveling faster."
Nonrestrictive and Parenthetical Elements Written Incorrectly	"On my very first trip—it was to Iowa, I slept the whole way. I woke up and asked what the white stuff, snow, was on the ground. My dad recited a poem, "Jack Frost" and laughed."
Nonrestrictive and Parenthetical Elements Written Correctly	"On my very first trip—it was to Iowa—I slept the whole way. I woke up and asked what the white stuff (snow) was on the ground. My dad recited a poem, "Jack Frost," and laughed."

The paragraph contains errors involving dialogue and nonrestrictive or paranthetical elements. Rewrite the paragraph with correct punctuation and paragraph breaks.

Caleb and Amanda got on the airplane and found their seats. "I can't believe I'm going to fly Amanda exclaimed. It's a mix of emotions, excitement and nervousness—all at once. "Me too said Caleb." What movie are they going to show, he asked. It's the new comedy, *Zany Zoo* I think. Amanda replied. Yay, Caleb cried That's supposed to be really good.

_____

_____

_____

_____

_____

_____

_____

Focus Trait: Elaboration
Using Standard English

Sentence with Nonstandard English	Sentence with Standard English
Harriet Quimby was a cool female pilot.	Harriet Quimby was an excellent female pilot.

A. Change the underlined word(s) in each sentence to standard English.

Sentence with Nonstandard English	Sentence with Standard English
Jacqueline Cochran, the first woman to fly a bomber jet across the Atlantic, was <u>super</u> brave.	
Benjamin Oliver Davis, Jr., <u>headed</u> <u>up</u> the first African-American military flying unit.	

B. Pair/Share Rewrite each sentence in standard English. Work with a partner to think of the best words.

Sentence with Nonstandard English	Sentence with Standard English
Samuel Pierpoint Langley was the first guy to get a gas-powered plane in the air.	
But Langley's totally forgotten because the thing crashed into a river.	
Something like nine days later, the Wright Brothers beat him to the punch.	

Name _____ Date _____

 Reader's Guide

Number the Stars

Design and Write a Postcard

In this passage, Annemarie travels to Denmark to stay with her uncle who is helping Jewish people escape to safety. Use evidence from the text to explain how Annemarie responds to key events.

Reread page 674. How does Annemarie respond to the German soldiers when they pick through the lunch basket?

_____

_____

_____

Reread page 675. How does Annemarie respond to the German soldiers when they discover the packet?

_____

_____

_____

Reread page 677. How does Annemarie respond when she reaches her uncle and does not see her friends?

_____

_____

_____

Think about Annemarie's experiences and her response to them. Suppose she wrote a postcard to her friend Ellen. What might she tell her friend? Remember she must be cautious in case someone sees her message.

Dear Ellen,
_____
_____
_____
_____
_____
_____
_____
_____
_____
_____

Ellen Rosen
Sweden

Friends Forever,
Annemarie

Name _____ Date _____

Lesson 23
READER'S NOTEBOOK

Number the Stars
Vocabulary Strategies:
Using Context

Using Context

Context clues may give a definition, provide an example for an unknown word, or help determine the correct meaning of a multiple-meaning word. Read each sentence below. Circle the words in the sentence that give clues to the meaning of the underlined word. Then write the meaning on the line. Use a dictionary to verify your meanings for the words.

1. Maggie begged the firefighters to save her dog. "Please do something," she implored.

   _____

2. Use of the Internet is widespread. It is prevalent around the world.

   _____

3. She was brave in the face of danger. She exhibited an immense amount of prowess.

   _____

4. My vision was obscured. The fog was too dense.

   _____

5. Tina threw the ball at Jeff and it glanced off of his shoulder.

   _____

6. The excited dog's bark sounded harsh in the distance. Up close, it was even more strident.

   _____

7. The moon shed silvery light onto the grass.

   _____

Name _____ Date _____

Suffixes: *-ic, -ure, -ous*

Basic Write the Basic Word that completes each analogy.

1. *greedy* is to *selfish* as *charitable* is to _____

2. *happy* is to *comedic* as *sad* is to _____

3. *painter* is to *painting* as *sculptor* is to _____

4. *kitten* is to *safe* as *rattlesnake* is to _____

5. *house* is to *small* as *castle* is to _____

6. *awful* is to *terrible* as *fabulous* is to _____

7. *steady* is to *calm* as *shaking* is to _____

8. *actor* is to *artistic* as *astronomer* is to _____

9. *Fourth of July* is to *patriotic* as *Valentine's Day*

   is to _____

10. *mend* is to *fuse* as *break* is to _____

11. *careless* is to *lazy* as *motivated* is to _____

12. *uninterested* is to *bored* as *interested* is to _____

Challenge The President of the United States makes many decisions about how the country is run. Write a short paragraph in which you are President for one day. Use four of the Challenge Words. Write on a separate sheet of paper.

Spelling Words

1. fantastic
2. culture
3. curious
4. nervous
5. posture
6. jealous
7. scientific
8. generous
9. signature
10. dangerous
11. tragic
12. gigantic
13. sculpture
14. precious
15. lecture
16. serious
17. specific
18. fracture
19. romantic
20. ambitious

Challenge
symbolic
unanimous
authentic
nutritious
legislature

Spelling Word Sort

Number the Stars
Spelling: Suffixes: *-ic, -ure, -ous*

Write each Basic Word beside the correct heading.

Suffix *-ic*	
Suffix *-ure*	
Suffix *-ous*	

Challenge   Add the Challenge Words to your Word Sort.

Connect to Reading   Look through *Number the Stars*. Find words with suffixes *-ic, -ure,* and *-ous*. Add them to your Word Sort.

Spelling Words

1. fantastic
2. culture
3. curious
4. nervous
5. posture
6. jealous
7. scientific
8. generous
9. signature
10. dangerous
11. tragic
12. gigantic
13. sculpture
14. precious
15. lecture
16. serious
17. specific
18. fracture
19. romantic
20. ambitious

Challenge
symbolic
unanimous
authentic
nutritious
legislature

Name _____ Date _____

Proofreading for Spelling

Find the misspelled words and circle them. Write them correctly on the lines below.

Dear Mama,

    I arrived tonight in the home of our generus friends, and they quickly led me to the room where I will be hiding. The trip here was so dangerus, but we arrived without sereous trouble. I am so nervus about being here. I am cureous about the world outside these walls. When I pull back the curtain at night, I see a sculpchure in the park and a jigantic building nearby. I am jealos of the people who can walk around in the fresh air. While a visit from you would be fanntastic, I know it is just an ambishus dream that I have. It would be trajic if I were discovered, so I'll follow your spesific directions to stay quiet and still. I'll dream of you and the preshous day when I will see you again.

                   Love,

                   Jenna

Spelling Words

1. fantastic
2. culture
3. curious
4. nervous
5. posture
6. jealous
7. scientific
8. generous
9. signature
10. dangerous
11. tragic
12. gigantic
13. sculpture
14. precious
15. lecture
16. serious
17. specific
18. fracture
19. romantic
20. ambitious

1. _____
2. _____
3. _____
4. _____
5. _____
6. _____
7. _____
8. _____
9. _____
10. _____
11. _____
12. _____
13. _____

Contractions with Pronouns

A **contraction** is a single word that is formed by combining two words, such as a pronoun and a verb. An apostrophe is used to indicate that a letter or letters have been taken out.

Thinking Question
Which letters should I leave out when combining the pronoun and the verb?

Without contraction	With contraction
You are a great pilot.	You're a great pilot.
It is time for take off.	It's time for take off.
We are flying overseas.	We're flying overseas.

Activity Combine the underlined pronouns and verbs to form contractions. Write your answer on the lines provided.

1. Let us fly over the airfield one more time. _____

2. He is looking for a place to land the plane. _____

3. Instead of landing the plane, we are returning to the carrier. _____

4. She has been working in the factory. _____

5. I know you are going to plant a Victory Garden. _____

6. They have never considered defeat. _____

Common Errors

Be careful not to confuse **contractions** with **possessive pronouns**.

Contraction	Possessive pronoun
<u>You're</u> an excellent captain.	<u>Your</u> brother is an excellent captain.
<u>It's</u> rewarding to be part of a unit.	The group practiced <u>its</u> drills.
<u>They're</u> bringing in a new commander.	The soldiers carried <u>their</u> gear into camp.

Thinking Question
Which word makes sense in the sentence: the word that shows possession or the word that combines two words?

Activity Read the sentences. Circle the correct contraction or possessive pronoun to complete each sentence.

1. Kade and Domenic forgot _____ marching boots.

   they're   their

2. _____ time to run through the plans for attack.

   Its   It's

3. Please bring _____ tags for identification.

   you're   your

4. If Casey and Andy don't make a plan, _____ not going to be able to rescue the prisoners.

   they're   their

5. I just know _____ going to be a hero!

   you're   your

6. My boot lost _____ lace.

   its   it's

Contractions with *not*

A **contraction** can be formed by combining a verb with the word *not*.

I cannot believe Marcia will not ration butter.

contractions

I can't believe Marcia won't ration butter.

Thinking Questions
Which word was made by combining two words? Which two words were combined to form it?

Activity Read the sentences. Underline the contractions. On the line provided, write the two words that were used to form the contraction.

1. We mustn't use rationed sugar wastefully. _____

2. Shannon hasn't found her ration book. _____

3. The gas tank doesn't need to be filled during this time of shortage. _____

4. Opal and Randy won't stop hanging signs that read, "I'm in this fight, too!" _____

5. Rationing isn't going to end until the war ends! _____

6. I missed my carpool to work because I couldn't tear myself away from the president's radio address about Pearl Harbor. _____

Adjectives and Adverbs

Adjectives	What Kind	The soldier had to cut his **shaggy** hair.
	Which One	**That** soldier had to shave his beard, too.
	How Many	**Most** soldiers like to eat home-cooked meals.
Adverbs	How	The captain called **loudly**.
	Where	The soldier stood **there**.
	When	**Then** he raised his hand in salute.
	To What Extent	David is **really** intent on shining his shoes.

1–3. Write each adjective and the word that it modifies.

1. Scott is an energetic soldier. _____

2. His face is caked with brown mud. _____

3. I tossed him a worn, tattered medal. _____

4–6. Write each adverb and the word that it modifies.

4. Scott quickly returned the medal. _____

5. For a small man, he throws surprisingly well. _____

6. This man is absolutely courageous. _____

7–8. Combine each pair of sentences by moving an adjective or adverb from one sentence to the other. Write your new sentence on the line.

7. Soldiers use their sense of hearing. Their sense of hearing is keen.

_____

8. If a soldier feels threatened, he may fight. He may fight ferociously.

_____

Name _____ Date _____

Connect to Writing

Incorrect	Correct
did'nt	didn't
its'	it's
theyr'e	they're

Read the sentence. Circle the contractions that are punctuated incorrectly.

Write the contraction using correct punctuation on the lines provided.

1. I feel proud of my service, so Im re-enlisting. _____

2. The unit doe'snt get a lot of recognition, but it should.

_____

3. Its wonderful that we rationed so many items. _____

4. Dont you know that wer'e being written about in the local paper?

_____

5. Youv'e got to see Paul's medals. _____

6. We must'nt worry about victory; we must believe in it! _____

Focus Trait: Purpose
Different Approaches to Persuasion

Logical Approach	Emotional Approach
The book won many awards.	The plot is tense and exciting.
It contains a wide variety of historical facts.	I really identified with the characters.
The characters are realistic and believable.	I bet you won't be able to put it down!

Read each claim on the left. In the right-hand column, tell whether the claim takes a logical or an emotional approach.

Claim	Approach
This science fiction novel tells about a future society, a subject that interests many people.	
I thought the book was fascinating and scary.	
The main character, Jonas, learns a lot of lessons that can teach the reader about life.	
I think readers will be amazed by the story and find lots of parallels to the way we live today.	

Write four claims a library might use to explain why Lois Lowry should be given an award. Use two logical approaches and two emotional approaches.

Logical Approach	Emotional Approach

Pair/Share Work with a partner to brainstorm reasons and evidence for your sentences.

Name _____ Date _____

Lesson 24
READER'S NOTEBOOK

Harriet Tubman
Independent Reading

Reader's Guide

Harriet Tubman: Conductor on the Underground Railroad

Design a Quilt

In this story, Harriet gives her special quilt to the kind woman who helped her at the beginning of her journey. Quilts often tell stories. Some were even made to show slaves how to escape. Design a quilt below. In each quilt block, draw part of Harriet's journey.

Reread pages 702–703. What does the author tell about Harriet's life before she escaped?

_____

_____

_____

_____

What do you think her purpose was in showing Harriet's life before her journey?

_____

_____

_____

_____

Reread pages 704–706. What do you think her purpose was in describing Harriet's brothers' thoughts towards running away?

_____

_____

_____

_____

Reread pages 710–715. The author tells about the different stops that Harriet makes along the Underground Railroad. What do you think her purpose is in describing each of these spots?

_____

_____

_____

Prefixes *con-, com-, pre-, pro-*

Choose the word that best completes each sentence. Then write the meaning of the word you chose. Use a dictionary to help, if needed.

congenial	confirm	compress	compile
preview	predetermine	proclaim	proactive

1. The friendly waitress had a _____ attitude.

   _____

2. My mom called the dentist's office to _____ my

   appointment. _____

3. Because we are _____ about keeping

   the park clean, it hasn't had a problem with litter.

   _____

4. The candidate walked to the microphone to _____ that

   she was planning to run for mayor. _____

5. We left early to _____ the show.

   _____

6. They hired a clerk to _____ a list of the survey results.

   _____

7. During planning, we used a map to _____ the length of

   our trip. _____

8. If you _____ a pillow, it can be stored in a small space.

   _____

Prefixes: *de-, trans-*

Basic Write the Basic Word that best fits each clue.

1. a written or printed copy of what people have said

   _____

2. to warm up, to melt _____

3. to tear apart _____

4. to freshen _____

5. to change appearance _____

6. an alternative route _____

7. to send from one place to another _____

8. to remove someone from power _____

9. to wreck or throw off-course _____

10. a business exchange _____

11. to discourage or dishearten _____

Challenge Write an article about your visit to the community botanical gardens or state park. Use three of the Challenge Words. Write on a separate sheet of paper.

Spelling Words

1. transform
2. deject
3. destruct
4. detour
5. transmit
6. default
7. describe
8. defend
9. transplant
10. descend
11. derail
12. defrost
13. transcript
14. deploy
15. dethrone
16. deodorize
17. transatlantic
18. decompose
19. decrease
20. transaction

Challenge
degenerate
transition
dehydrate
transfusion
translucent

Name _____ Date _____

Spelling Word Sort

Write each Basic Word beside the correct heading.

Prefix *de-*	
Prefix *trans-*	

Challenge Add the Challenge Words to your Word Sort.

Connect to Reading Look through *Harriet Tubman.* Find words that have the prefixes *de-* or *trans-* . Add them to your Word Sort.

Spelling Words

1. transform
2. deject
3. destruct
4. detour
5. transmit
6. default
7. describe
8. defend
9. transplant
10. descend
11. derail
12. defrost
13. transcript
14. deploy
15. dethrone
16. deodorize
17. transatlantic
18. decompose
19. decrease
20. transaction

Challenge
degenerate
transition
dehydrate
transfusion
translucent

Name _____ Date _____

Proofreading for Spelling

Find the misspelled words and circle them. Write them correctly on the lines below.

Jim rushed home to tell his family about his day. When saw his mom trying to difrost the freezer, he took a detoor around the kitchen and headed upstairs to duhscribe his day to his father. He wished he had a transkript of what had happened because he had forgotten so many details.

"Watch where you're going!" his sister exclaimed. Jim didn't notice that he was about to derale her as she tried to desend the staircase.

He tried to diffend himself. "Sorry! It's been such a strange day!" Even his clumsiness couldn't decreese his confidence, though. Jim had been a shy tranzplan at his new school. The tranzatlantik move had been a big adjustment, and he sometimes thought he would distruc . After today, though, Jim felt like a million bucks. Despite his shyness, he had decided to try something new this week, and it had paid off in a big way. Jim had landed the lead role in the school musical! After his first attempt to diploy his singing voice, he realized he had a great talent!

Spelling Words

1. transform
2. deject
3. destruct
4. detour
5. transmit
6. default
7. describe
8. defend
9. transplant
10. descend
11. derail
12. defrost
13. transcript
14. deploy
15. dethrone
16. deodorize
17. transatlantic
18. decompose
19. decrease
20. transaction

1. _____ 7. _____

2. _____ 8. _____

3. _____ 9. _____

4. _____ 10. _____

5. _____ 11. _____

6. _____ 12. _____

Comparing with Adjectives

The **comparative form** (*-er*) of an adjective is used to compare two people, places, things, or ideas. The **superlative form** (*-est*) is used to compare three or more. Sometimes the spelling of an adjective changes when *-er* or *-est* is added.

comparative form

Tuesday night's applause at the rally was <u>louder</u> than Monday's.

superlative form

Tuesday night's applause at the rally was surely the <u>loudest</u> of the entire year.

Thinking Questions
Does this word compare two things or more than two things? Do I add -er or -est to make this comparison?

Activity Write the correct comparative or superlative form of the adjective in parentheses to complete the sentence.

1. This was the (great) concert of her career. _____

2. This protest rally is (long) than any other that I've attended. _____

3. I'm (happy) now than I've ever been because equality seems possible.

   _____

4. I caught the (early) train I could to arrive at the Lincoln Memorial for
   Dr. King's speech. _____

5. The news of Dr. King's death made me (sad) than it made her.

   _____

6. Dr. Martin Luther King, Jr., was the (wise) man I knew.

   _____

Name _____ Date _____

Other Adjective Comparisons

More is used to form the **comparative** and *most* to form the **superlative** of many two-syllable adjectives, all adjectives of three or more syllables, and all adjectives ending in -ed. Some adjectives have **different forms** in the comparative and superlative.

Thinking Question
What are the adjective comparisons in this sentence?

superlative

That was the best freedom concert I have ever heard.

The words *less* and *least* may also be used to show comparison of adjectives.

comparative

I was less interested in the protest speech than my parents were.

Activity Write the correct comparative or superlative form of the adjective in parentheses to complete the sentence.

1. I admire her because she is the (modest) performer I know.

   _____

2. I have never heard a (good) voice. _____

3. The song "Oh Freedom" is even (beautiful) than that one.

   _____

4. My birthday was the (pleasant) day of the year because I shook hands with Dr. King. _____

5. It was the (bad) downpour she had seen since the march to Washington began. _____

6. The rally audience was quieter and (enthusiastic) today than it was yesterday. _____

Comparing with Adverbs

To form the comparative form of many **adverbs**, add *-er*, and to form the superlative form, add *-est*. For adverbs that end with *-ly*, add *more* or *less* to form the comparative, and add *most* or *least* to form the superlative.

I rode the freedom bus far. Hannah rode the freedom bus farther.
Jay rode the freedom bus the farthest.
I shouted enthusiastically. Hannah shouted more enthusiastically. Jay shouted most enthusiastically.

Thinking Question
Does this adverb end in -ly? Should I change the ending or add a word to make it comparative or superlative?

Activity Write the correct comparative or superlative form of the word in parentheses to complete the sentence.

1. I got to the protest rally (late) than Ben did.

   _____

2. The guard with the blue coat raced around the crowd (frantic) than

   the others. _____

3. The speaker at the podium looked at us (stern) for talking than the

   previous speaker had. _____

4. Out of the whole group, Mary sat (quiet) during the rally.

   _____

5. Amber sat (close) to the speaker and farthest from the crowd.

   _____

6. Deirdre spoke (excited) than Amber about the Civil Rights Movement.

   _____

Prepositions

Prepositions	
prepositional phrase	The age **of intelligent protest** is here.
preposition	The age **of** intelligent protest is here.
object of preposition	The age of intelligent **protest** is here.
modifier of object	The age of **intelligent** protest is here.

adjective phrase	Dr. King was a civil rights leader **from America.**
adverb phrase	Dr. King traveled **to India.**

1–3.   Read each sentence. Underline the preposition once and the object of the preposition twice. Then circle the word or words that the phrase modifies.

  1. Volunteers from the North worked in the South.

  2. They rode in buses and cars.

  3. Generations of people have fought for civil rights.

4–5.   **Combine the sentence pairs.**

  4. Protest organizers wanted help with sit-ins. They wanted help from college students.

  _____

  _____

  5. Organizers worked on plans in secret. They worked on plans for nonviolent protest.

  _____

  _____

Connect to Writing

Adjective	Comparative	Superlative
tiny	tinier	tiniest
forceful	more forceful	most forceful
good	better	best

Adverb	Comparative	Superlative
frequently	more frequently	most frequently
clearly	less clearly	least clearly
far	farther	farthest

Read the sentences. Underline the incorrect comparative/superlative forms. Write the correct forms on the lines provided.

1. The church holds civil rights rallies more oftener than our

   government. _____

2. The audience watched attentiver when they heard angry shouting

   outside the church. _____

3. Tears of anger and despair are the saltyest I've ever tasted.

   _____

4. Of all parts of the rally, the crowd cheered loudly when Dr. King

   stepped on stage. _____

5. Wendell thought the concert was the most good part of the rally.

   _____

6. The Freedom Singers are the talentedest performers I know.

   _____

Focus Trait: Evidence

Supporting a Claim with Reasons and Evidence

Writers of strong arguments know how to support a claim with clear reasons and relevant evidence. Evidence can take the form of facts, details, examples, and quotations from credible sources.

Claim
The school vending machine should sell only healthful snacks.

Reason
Childhood obesity is on the rise.

Evidence
(Fact) In the past thirty years, obesity in school-age children has increased from 7 percent to 20 percent.

Read each claim and reason. Then, write an example of evidence that will strongly support the reason.

1. **Claim:** The library should remain open later than 2:00 PM on Saturdays.

   Reason: Kids often need the use of library resources on Saturday afternoons.

   Evidence: _____

   _____

2. **Claim:** Students in our school should wear uniforms.

   Reason: Kids spend too much money on clothing.

   Evidence: _____

   _____

3. **Claim:** Students should be allowed to have cell phones at our school.

   Reason: Parents often need to contact their children about emergency situations.

   Evidence: _____

   _____

Name _____ Date _____

 Reader's Guide

Robotics

Think Like an Engineer

Find evidence to show what engineering challenges each robot has overcome and what it has contributed to the field of engineering.

Reread the third paragraph on page 734 and all of page 735.

Robot:	
What challenges did the robot face? How did it overcome them?	**What has it contributed to the field of robotics?**
_____	_____

Reread page 736.

Robots:	
What challenges did the robots face? How did they overcome these challenges?	**What have they contributed to the field of robotics?**
_____	_____

Reread the second and third paragraphs on page 737.

Robots:	
What challenges did the robots face? How did they overcome these challenges?	What have they contributed to the field of robotics?
_____ _____ _____ _____	_____ _____ _____ _____

Read the second and third paragraphs on page 743.

Robot:	
What challenges did the robot face? How did it overcome them?	What has it contributed to the field of robotics?
_____ _____ _____ _____	_____ _____ _____ _____

Think about the advances made by each of these robots. What do you think they tell us about the future of robotics?

_____

_____

_____

Suffixes *-able, -ible*

The words in the box end in a suffix that means "can" or "able to."
Choose the word that best completes each sentence.

legible	disputable	audible	collapsible	edible
predictable	advisable	compatible	memorable	capable

1. The sloppy writing was not _____.

2. Do you think it is _____ to wear a gown to a pool party?

3. Although he was hungry, he was unsure whether the fruit was

   _____.

4. It was _____ whether or not the man was guilty.

5. I couldn't hear the singer; she was barely _____.

**Now use the remaining words to write five new sentences that show you
know the meaning of the words.**

6. _____

   _____

7. _____

   _____

8. _____

   _____

9. _____

   _____

10. _____

   _____

Word Parts

Basic Read the paragraph. Write the Basic Word that best replaces the underlined word or words in the sentences.

The **(1)** <u>planning</u> of my school's annual talent show began with the planning committee. Committee members gave us **(2)** <u>facts</u> about tryout dates and times. The audition I had with my friend Jack went **(3)** <u>flawlessly</u>, and we made the show! Weeks of **(4)** <u>getting ready</u> helped us to feel ready to perform. **(5)** <u>The turnout</u> was quite high, with parents and students present. The level of excitement backstage was **(6)** <u>astonishing</u>. Several students showed intense **(7)** <u>focus</u> before their performances. After an hour of entertainment, there was a(n) **(8)** <u>break</u>. We had some **(9)** <u>snacks</u> as we talked about the acts. Jack and I agreed that there was great **(10)** <u>progress</u> compared with last year's show.

1. _____   6. _____

2. _____   7. _____

3. _____   8. _____

4. _____   9. _____

5. _____   10. _____

Challenge Write a paragraph about a career choice—for example, a teacher, a lawyer, a carpenter, or an architect. Give reasons for your choice. Use three of the Challenge Words. Write on a separate sheet of paper.

Spelling Words

1. existence
2. refreshment
3. convention
4. intermission
5. uneventful
6. perfectly
7. completion
8. improvement
9. information
10. attendance
11. reversible
12. invention
13. development
14. respectful
15. unhappiness
16. preparation
17. irrigate
18. disagreement
19. unbelievable
20. concentration

Challenge
acquaintance
prosecution
precision
immeasurable
reputation

Spelling Word Sort

Write each Basic Word beside the correct heading.

Three-syllable words	
Four-syllable words	
Five-syllable words	

Challenge   Add the Challenge Words to your Word Sort.

Connect to Reading   Look through *Robotics.* Find words that have a prefix, a base word or word root, and a suffix. Add them to your Word Sort.

Spelling Words

1. existence
2. refreshment
3. convention
4. intermission
5. uneventful
6. perfectly
7. completion
8. improvement
9. information
10. attendance
11. reversible
12. invention
13. development
14. respectful
15. unhappiness
16. preparation
17. irrigate
18. disagreement
19. unbelievable
20. concentration

Challenge
acquaintance
prosecution
precision
immeasurable
reputation

Name _____ Date _____

Proofreading for Spelling

Find the misspelled words and circle them. Write them correctly on the lines below.

The innvention of industrial robots was always seen as an impprovement by some and a threat by others. Today, each convenntion that doesn't announce the developpment of new models is usually an uneventfull one. But throughout history, the compleetion of every machine that replaced human workers has been met with some unhapiness and disaggreement. People are afraid that they will lose their jobs, and they are often right. Even something as simple as a timer to irigate fields meant that someone no longer did that job by hand. Now that robots have come into exisstance, this trend is not reversable. Companies that introduce robots try to be respectfull of workers' fears, but the end result is always the same. The machines will be made and used, and workers must adjust.

Spelling Words

1. existence
2. refreshment
3. convention
4. intermission
5. uneventful
6. perfectly
7. completion
8. improvement
9. information
10. attendance
11. reversible
12. invention
13. development
14. respectful
15. unhappiness
16. preparation
17. irrigate
18. disagreement
19. unbelievable
20. concentration

1. _____ 7. _____
2. _____ 8. _____
3. _____ 9. _____
4. _____ 10. _____
5. _____ 11. _____
6. _____ 12. _____

Robotics
Grammar: Proper Mechanics

Sentence Types: End Punctuation

There are three types of **end punctuation** that conclude a sentence: the period, the question mark, and the exclamation point. The most common is the period, which ends a sentence that makes a statement. A question mark is used for a question, and an exclamation point is used to convey strong emotion.

statement
I went to the store today.

question
Did you go to the store today?

exclamation
I was so excited to go to the store today!

Thinking Question
Does this sentence make a statement, ask a question, or express strong emotion?

Activity Write the correct punctuation at the end of each sentence.

1. A robot is mechanical _____

2. I can't believe the robot looked so real _____

3. Who designed the first robot _____

4. Bobby was thrilled to start reading the story _____

5. Did you finish writing the report _____

6. Many robots use electric motors _____

7. Today, robots are commonly used to perform certain jobs for humans _____

8. What an amazing invention _____

Interjections: Punctuation

An **interjection** is a word or group of words that expresses emotion. An interjection that expresses very strong feeling is followed by an exclamation point. An interjection that expresses mild feeling is followed by a comma and appears at the beginning of a sentence.

exclamation point

Yay! I'm excited for the trip.

comma

Oh, I didn't know we weren't leaving until tomorrow.

Thinking Questions
Is this a strong emotional expression that is separate from the next sentence? Or does it express milder emotion and begin a sentence?

Activity   Add a comma or exclamation point after each underlined interjection.

1. Hooray I passed the test.
2. Oh no it's too late to study.
3. Wow I got to see a real robot.
4. Yikes It looks like an alien.
5. Fine we can wait to see the exhibit.
6. Ouch I stubbed my toe on the way to the bus.
7. Phew We have bandages in the first aid kit.
8. Oh there's time to have lunch before we leave.

Capitalization: Proper Nouns and Proper Adjectives

A **proper noun** names a specific person, place, or thing, and begins with a capital letter. A **proper adjective** is often derived from a proper noun and also begins with a capital letter.

proper noun

I went on a trip to <u>China</u>.

proper adjective

I ate <u>Chinese</u> food there.

Thinking Questions
Is this word the name of a person, place, or thing? Is it derived from the name of a person, place, or thing and does it begin with a capital letter?

Activity Underline the proper noun or proper adjective in each sentence.

1. The first descriptions of machines were made by Heron of Alexandria.
2. George Devol received a patent for the first commercial robot.
3. Japanese mechanical toys were made in the 1800s.
4. Even Leonardo da Vinci had made a design for a robot.
5. The term "robot" was coined by a Czech writer.
6. His name was Karel Čapek.
7. He used the word in a play called *Rossum's Universal Robots*.
8. His brother Josef was a painter.

Using Adjectives and Adverbs

Nonrestrictive Element	The robots, all of which are based on insects, are very small.
Parenthetical Elements	The largest robot—known as Atlas—stood seven feet tall.
	Tiny robots may one day be able to make people better (by removing plaque from arteries, for example).

1–6. Look for the nonrestrictive or parenthetical element in each sentences below. Rewrite the sentence on the line with correct punctuation.

1. This is my strongest robot SAM.

   _____

2. I made him when I was 12 two years ago.

   _____

3. He helps me I'm happy to say by lifting heavy things.

   _____

4. There are smarter robots don't tell him.

   _____

5. But SAM who was my first will always be special to me.

   _____

6. He lives with me in my room in my closet, specifically.

   _____

7–8. Use a nonrestrictive or parenthetical element to add information to each sentence. Write the new sentence on the lines.

7. The robot head looked at me from the table.

   _____

   _____

8. Its eyes seemed strangely human.

   _____

Connect to Writing

When you proofread your writing, you must make a habit of checking for correct punctuation and capitalization.

incorrect punctuation	incorrect capitalization
Hooray, that was the best movie I've ever seen.	brian brought back souvenirs from russia.
correct punctuation	**correct capitalization**
Hooray! That was the best movie I've ever seen!	Brian brought back souvenirs from Russia.

Read each sentence. Then write the sentence correctly on the lines provided.

1. Are you reading that book!

   _____

2. I'm going to build robots in south america.

   _____

3. jane said she had been there before.

   _____

4. Cool, it sounds amazing.

   _____

5. I'm especially looking forward to visiting peru.

   _____

6. From there, we go to silicon valley.

   _____

Focus Trait: Elaboration
Using Persuasive Language

Statement	More Persuasive Statement
People are afraid that robots may be too smart and a threat to humanity.	People have imagined the possibility of highly intelligent robots taking over the human race. This fear has been expressed in countless books and films, from science fiction novels to action movies.

Fill in the blanks with words that are more persuasive than the examples on the left. Choose words that are confident, positive, and convincing.

Instead of this...	you can write this.
1. Modern technology can do things that help some people.	Modern technology can _____ that help _____ people.
2. Fooling around with robots has probably had many big results.	_____ robots has _____ _____ results.

Rewrite each sentence to make it more persuasive. Change or add persuasive language, and eliminate words that are vague or sound uncertain.

3. Robots might help doctors take care of people.

_____

_____

4. People will usually like a robot more if it looks like it has expressions.

_____

_____

5. A few people are putting together robots that are actually really small.

_____

_____

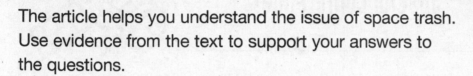

Space Trash

Design a Poster

The article helps you understand the issue of space trash.
Use evidence from the text to support your answers to
the questions.

**Read the last paragraph on page 4. What evidence shows that space
trash is a problem?**

_____

_____

_____

**Review the information on pages 4, 5, and 6. What contributes to the
space trash problem?**

_____

_____

_____

Read page 8. Why is space trash a concern?

_____

_____

_____

Suppose scientists are holding a special conference to discuss the issue of space trash. Design a poster to advertise the conference.

You Are Invited to Attend a Special Conference!

_____

Why this issue is important:

_____

_____

_____

Topics to be discussed:

_____

_____

_____

What scientists have to say about this conference:

_____

_____

_____

Words from Other Languages

Basic Write the Basic Word that matches each clue.

1. a place to eat _____

2. the only one of its kind _____

3. a group of animals running wild _____

4. a festival or celebration _____

5. flying insect that bites _____

6. a type of school or college _____

7. a violent storm with strong winds and a funnel-shaped

cloud _____

8. an older object _____

9. a type of poem _____

10. exhaustion or tiredness _____

11. not clear or specific _____

12. document that you receive when you graduate

_____

13. booklet _____

14. dramatic work with most lines sung instead of spoken

_____

Challenge Imagine that you and a friend have met on Florida's coast to look for buried treasure, and you find a Spanish treasure chest buried in the sand. Use four of the Challenge Words to describe your adventure. Write on a separate sheet of paper.

Spelling Words

1. opera
2. vague
3. antique
4. drama
5. tornado
6. debut
7. stampede
8. gourmet
9. unique
10. academy
11. sonnet
12. brochure
13. cocoon
14. fatigue
15. mosquito
16. diploma
17. fiesta
18. debris
19. cafeteria
20. quartet

Challenge
bonanza
rendezvous
et cetera
battalion
engage

Spelling Word Sort

Write each Basic Word beside the correct heading. Use a dictionary to help you.

Italian	
French	
Greek or Latin	
Spanish	

Challenge   Add the Challenge Words to your Word Sort.

Spelling Words

1. opera
2. vague
3. antique
4. drama
5. tornado
6. debut
7. stampede
8. gourmet
9. unique
10. academy
11. sonnet
12. brochure
13. cocoon
14. fatigue
15. mosquito
16. diploma
17. fiesta
18. debris
19. cafeteria
20. quartet

Challenge
bonanza
rendezvous
et cetera
battalion
engage

Name _____ Date _____

Lesson 26
READER'S NOTEBOOK

Proofreading for Spelling

Space Trash
Spelling: Words from Other Languages

Find the misspelled words and circle them. Write them correctly on the lines below.

Spelling Words

1. opera
2. vague
3. antique
4. drama
5. tornado
6. debut
7. stampede
8. gourmet
9. unique
10. academy
11. sonnet
12. brochure
13. cocoon
14. fatigue
15. mosquito
16. diploma
17. fiesta
18. debris
19. cafeteria
20. quartet

If a class could earn a group duploma, this class would get one for creativity. Feeling elated from the success of their mini-silkworm project, the students decided to write a light opura about it. Derek's vaugue plot, set in China 5,000 years ago, involved the harvest of the silkworm cacoon, not exactly what you'd find in an action dramuh. A qartet in anteque silk robes on loan from the art acadamy would sing a sonet they wrote. Wanda designed an ad broshure. The principal agreed to let the class use the stage in the cafuteria for the debue if they would clean up the lunchtime debree for the week. Kim and Sharad baked gormay cookies to sell at intermission. The town didn't actually form a stampeed to the show, but it was a fitting end to an enterprising year.

1. _____ 9. _____
2. _____ 10. _____
3. _____ 11. _____
4. _____ 12. _____
5. _____ 13. _____
6. _____ 14. _____
7. _____ 15. _____
8. _____

Spelling   353   Grade 6, Unit 6
© Houghton Mifflin Harcourt Publishing Company. All rights reserved.

Writing Titles: Capitalization and Italics/Underlining

- Capitalize the first, last, and all important words in a **title**.

- Underline titles of major works, such as **books, magazines, newspapers**, and **movies**. (When typing, use italics instead of underlining.)

- Place quotation marks around titles of shorter works, such as **short stories, articles, songs, book chapters**, and most **poems**.

The story "The Lost Colony of Alpha Tara" was published in the magazine Science Fiction Today.

Thinking Questions
Is it the title of a long or short work? Which words in the title are important?

1–4. **Underline the title of a long work or place quotation marks around the title of a short work in each sentence. Then write the title on the line with correct capitalization and punctuation.**

1. Have you read the novel my best friend james?

   _____

2. I read the article In space, trash can't go to the curb for my science class.

   _____

3. I enjoy reading the magazine New scientist.

   _____

4. For tomorrow, read Chapter 4, The Earth And The Sun.

   _____

5–6. **Circle the typewritten title that is written correctly.**

5. At camp we learned folk songs such as "Blowin' in the Wind."
   At camp we learned folk songs such as *Blowin' in the Wind.*

6. If you like baseball, you'll love the book the *Home run Hitter.*
   If you like baseball, you'll love the book *The Home Run Hitter.*

Writing Titles: Quotation Marks

Place quotation marks around titles of short works such as **short stories, articles, songs,** or **poems.**

Place quotation marks around the title of part of a larger work such as **a book chapter, episode** in a series, or part of a longer **musical** or **piece of art.**

Jim is always humming "The Duck" from Peter and the Wolf.
My favorite chapter from Little House in the Big Woods is "The Wolf Pack."

Thinking Question
Is it the title of a short work?

Activity Place quotation marks around the title of the short work in each sentence. Underline the title of any longer works.

1. I read the poem Do Not Go Gentle into That Good Night, by Dylan Thomas.

2. Do you know The Star-Spangled Banner by heart?

3. It took me months to read Pride and Prejudice, a Jane Austen novel.

4. My favorite part is Chapter 5, A Happy Family.

5. My latest article, The Planet Mars, was published in the newspaper.

6. I was too scared to see the movie The Birds.

7. Katherine Anne Porter's Pale Horse, Pale Rider is a great short story.

8. The collection was titled The Complete Poems of Emily Dickinson.

Writing Abbreviations

An **abbreviation** is a shortened form of a word. Many abbreviations begin with a capital letter and end with a period.

The letter was addressed to **Dr**. James Smith, 1215 **S**. Hampton **Ave**., Paris, **IL**.

Thinking Question
What word could these letters logically represent?

1–7. Circle the abbreviation in each sentence. Spell out the word or words it represents. Item 7 contains two abbreviations.

1. The satellite is 2.5 m long. _____

2. Pick up the mail in P.O. Box 4915. _____

3. The store is located on Hwy. 38. _____

4. Gov. Alan Thompson is our speaker. _____

5. The shuttle slowed to 1200 mph. _____

6. We named our business Cocoa, Inc. _____

7. Mr. Smith and Dr. Jones are coming. _____

8–13. Create the abbreviation for each item below.

8. Illinois _____

9. Mount McKinley _____

10. Apartment 302 _____

11. East Second Avenue _____

12. 4 feet, 6 inches _____

13. January _____

Verb Phrases and Contractions

Verb Phrase		Example	
Helping Verb	Main Verb	Full form	Contracted form
have	sent	We <u>have sent</u> many objects into space.	We<u>'ve sent</u> many objects into space.
are	circling	They <u>are circling</u> Earth	They<u>'re circling</u> Earth.
will	lose	They <u>will lose</u> velocity someday.	They<u>'ll lose</u> velocity someday.
am	watching	I <u>am watching</u> the night sky.	I<u>'m watching</u> the night sky.

1–6. Underline the verb phrase in each sentence. Circle the helping verb. Remember that a helping verb may be part of a contraction.

1. Every satellite will become space trash one day.

2. They'll launch a rocket later today.

3. We've sent objects into space for many reasons.

4. Someday, humans could vacation in space.

5. Today, it's becoming a reality for more people.

6. She's piloted the shuttle around the space junk.

7–10. Underline the correct verb phrase in parentheses to complete each sentence.

7. What (is held, is holding) space junk in orbit?

8. The force of gravity (has pull, is pulling) objects in orbit toward Earth.

9. Orbiting objects (must travel, be traveling) 17,000 mph.

10. When they slow down, they (could pull, are pulled) to Earth by gravity.

Connect to Writing

Sentence with Errors in the Capitalization or Punctuation of Title	Sentence with Correctly Written Title
Brian Duffy wrote the article Lost in Space for our school paper, the franklin times.	Brian Duffy wrote the article "Lost in Space" for our school paper, The Franklin Times.

Sentence with Abbreviation Errors	Sentence with Correctly Written Abbreviations
Send the package to 25 Glidden Bld., Smithville, Mass.	Send the package to 25 Glidden Blvd., Smithville, MA.

Activity Rewrite each sentence using correct capitalization and punctuation for titles and correct abbreviations.

1. Would National geographic be a good source for a report titled Space Travel?

_____

_____

2. I would like to read this book, My life as an Astronaut, while I wait.

_____

_____

3. The jet travels an average speed of 500 mi. p. hr.

_____

_____

4. Are there peaks on Mars that are as tall as Mnt Everest?

_____

_____

Focus Trait: Elaboration

Vivid words create images in a reader's mind. Alliteration repeats beginning sounds in words for rhythm or flow. Choose words for the way they sound and the mood they create. For example, smooth-sounding words can create a peaceful mood, while rough- or choppy-sounding words can create a harsh effect.

Alliteration	The space shuttle sliced through the starry skies.
Smooth	Earth's seas looked blue and calm from space.
Choppy	Sharp peaks jutted from the rocky moonscape.

Rewrite each sentence to add alliteration.

1. The stars were bright.	
2. The moon had a rough surface.	

Rewrite each sentence, using smoother-sounding words.

3. The astronauts were weightless.	
4. They looked out at space.	

Rewrite each sentence, using choppier-sounding words.

5. We saw the tail of a comet.	
6. The space trash hit the spacecraft.	

Denali Dog Sled Journal

Write a Ranger Report and Job Description

The park ranger kept a journal chronicling her experiences on patrol. When she returned, she completed a report to summarize her patrol. Use evidence from the text to complete her report.

Denali National Park Dog Sled Patrol Report
Read the entry for December 9. Date: _____ Activities: _____ _____
Read the entry for December 10. Date: _____ Activities: _____ _____
Read the entry for December 11. Date: _____ Activities: _____ _____
Read the entry for December 12. Date: _____ Activities: _____ _____
Read the entries on p. 23. Date: _____ Activities: _____ _____

Use the activities from the ranger report to help you write a
job description for a park ranger at Denali National Park.

Park Ranger
Job Qualifications

Qualified applicants should have the following skills:

_____

_____

_____

Qualified applicants should have knowledge in the following subjects:

_____

_____

_____

Name _____ Date _____

Greek Word Parts

Basic Write the Basic Word that best fits each clue.

1. the study of what makes up the earth _____

2. a container that keeps liquids warm _____

3. a request to be forgiven _____

4. a list of events in time order _____

5. study of stories that try to explain beliefs or natural events, usually with imaginary characters _____

6. another name for a car _____

7. the study, creation, and use of machines and devices _____

8. a collection by one or more authors of various stories, books, or poems _____

9. a member of the upper class _____

10. self-activating _____

11. the math of points, lines, surfaces, and shapes

_____

Challenge You are part of a group of archaeology students on a dig looking for ancient artifacts in another country. Write a letter to your parents describing your experience. Use at least three of the Challenge Words. Write on a separate sheet of paper.

Spelling Words

1. geography
2. democracy
3. microbiology
4. technology
5. thermos
6. automatic
7. mythology
8. democratic
9. thermometer
10. chronology
11. automobile
12. aristocrat
13. thermal
14. geology
15. aristocracy
16. geometry
17. anthology
18. apology
19. thermostat
20. psychology

Challenge
archaeology
geographic
bureaucracy
etymology
autocrat

Spelling Word Sort

Denali Dog Sled Journal
Spelling: Greek Word Parts

Write each Basic Word beside the correct heading.

Words with *geo-*	
Words with *-crat* or *-cracy*	
Words with *-logy*	
Words with *therm-*	
Words with *auto-*	

Challenge Add the Challenge Words to your Word Sort.

Spelling Words

1. geography
2. democracy
3. microbiology
4. technology
5. thermos
6. automatic
7. mythology
8. democratic
9. thermometer
10. chronology
11. automobile
12. aristocrat
13. thermal
14. geology
15. aristocracy
16. geometry
17. anthology
18. apology
19. thermostat
20. psychology

Challenge
archaeology
geographic
bureaucracy
etymology
autocrat

Name _____ Date _____

Proofreading for Spelling

Find the misspelled words and circle them. Write them correctly on the lines below.

I love writing to my Internet pen pal, Mei. She lives in China and is my age. Mei is very curious about what American students learn in school. It's so great that tecknology allows us to chat, despite the giography that separates us.

I told her that we have been reading an antholegy about Greek mytholagy in our reading class. Mei told me that her favorite subjects are math and science, specifically geomatry and micro-biology. I told her that in science, we are studying geolegy and thirmal energy. We did an experiment using a thermoneter and the lab's thermestat.

In reviewing the cronology of our chats, I realized that I forgot to tell her that I would like to study psycology when I'm older.

It sure would be great to meet Mei in person one day!

Spelling Words

1. geography
2. democracy
3. microbiology
4. technology
5. thermos
6. automatic
7. mythology
8. democratic
9. thermometer
10. chronology
11. automobile
12. aristocrat
13. thermal
14. geology
15. aristocracy
16. geometry
17. anthology
18. apology
19. thermostat
20. psychology

1. _____   7. _____
2. _____   8. _____
3. _____   9. _____
4. _____   10. _____
5. _____   11. _____
6. _____   12. _____

Writing Direct and Indirect Quotations

> A **direct quotation** tells a speaker's exact
> words. The speaker's words are set off
> with **quotation marks**.
>
> **Thinking Question**
> *Which words are being spoken by someone?*
>
> • Place quotation marks around the speaker's words.
> • Capitalize the first word of the quotation.
> • Use a comma to separate the speaker from the quotation.
> • Place punctuation marks inside the ending quotation mark.
>
> I said, "I have never ridden on a dog sled."
>
> An **indirect quotation** paraphrases, or tells in other words,
> what the speaker said. Quotation marks are not used.
>
> John said that he had a lot of homework to do.

Activity Rewrite each sentence, using correct punctuation and capitalization.

1. We are going to Denali National Park today said Luca.

   _____

2. Ms. Turner told us "To take warm clothing."

   _____

3. Will we be able to hike in the park asked Leshaun.

   _____

4. Ms. Turner replied The snow is too deep for that.

   _____

5. Luca wondered, "if it would be a good day for skiing."

   _____

6. Luca asked Could we use cross-country skis?

   _____

Divided Quotations and Dialogue

> **Thinking Question**
> *What direct quotation is interrupted?*

- A **quotation** may be divided in the middle.
- Place **quotation marks** around both parts of the divided quotation.
- Use **commas** to separate the quotation from words that tell what the speaker is doing.

  "What on earth," asked Will, "is making that noise?"

Dialogue is a written conversation between two or more people. Start a new paragraph each time the speaker changes. Be sure the reader knows who is speaking.

  "Oh, what an eerie sound!" exclaimed Cam.
  "I think that is a wolf howling," said Inez.

1–3. Rewrite each sentence correctly.

1. I wonder said Cam how tall that mountain is.

_____

2. It is 20,320 feet tall said Will and it is called Mount McKinley.

_____

3. Do you think asked Inez that many people climb to the top?

_____

4–7. Read the following dialogue. Rewrite it with correct punctuation and paragraph breaks.

I'm getting really cold said Inez. There should be a cabin up ahead, replied Will.
Great cried Cam will it have heat?

_____

_____

_____

Question Marks and Exclamations Points

Question marks and exclamation points, like commas and periods, are always placed inside quotation marks in dialogue.

"You can do it!" cried the cheerleader.

"Are you sure?" he asked.

Thinking Question
Which words are being spoken by someone, and where does the punctuation go?

Activity Rewrite each sentence correctly.

1. Mary asked when will we reach the mountain peak

   _____

2. John cried I think I see the top

   _____

3. Is that step slippery I wondered

   _____

4. Whose backpack is this our guide asked

   _____

5. We'll never make it Mary exclaimed

   _____

6. Who's giving up so soon asked Fred

   _____

7. Not me John called out

   _____

8. I asked myself can I make it

   _____

Easily Confused Words

Confusing Pairs	Difference in Meaning	Sentence
sit	to rest in an upright position	I always sit in this chair.
set	to put or place an object	Mom set her cup down.
lie	to rest or recline	I lie down every afternoon for a nap.
lay	to put or place an object	I lay down my heavy load.
rise	to get up or go up	Rise early and watch the sun rise.
raise	to move something up, to grow something, or to increase	Raise your hand if you raise vegetables. They raised the price.
accept	(v.) to take something offered or given	I accept your kind offer. You may have any color car
except	(prep.) leaving out	except pink.
affect	(v.) to influence	Advice may affect a decision.
effect	(n.) a consequence or result	The effect of the ice was devastating.

1–6. **Underline the correct word in parentheses to complete each sentence.**

1. The cold (affects, effects) every living thing in Denali National Park.

2. The sled dogs like to (lay, lie) in a cave in the snow to keep warm.

3. The sun will (raise, rise) low on the horizon.

4. The musher may (set, sit) on the sled or stand next to it.

5. Mountain climbers (raise, rise) a flag at the top of the peak.

6. They (accept, except) any challenge in their quest.

7–10. **Correct the errors in these sentences. Underline each incorrect word and write the correct word on the line. There is one incorrect word in each sentence.**

7. The cabin is sit deep in the woods. _____

8. A friendly curl of smoke raises from its chimney. _____

9. You may lie your backpacks on the floor by the door. _____

10. The warmth of the fire has a soothing affect on cold, weary travelers. _____

Connect to Writing

Using direct quotations in combination with careful word choice can help vary sentence structure and create a lively, strong voice.

Sentence with Indirect Quotation	Sentence with Direct Quotation
Quinn said that all dogs should get special food.	Quinn stated emphatically, "All dogs should get special food."

Activity Rewrite each indirect quotation as a direct quotation. Change the verb that tells what the speaker is doing if you think it improves the sentence.

1. The ranger told us that the dogs eat a special food rich in protein, fats, and vitamins.

   _____

   _____

2. Nicolo said that no one is allowed to take cars into the park.

   _____

   _____

3. Andy said that the park feels like an ancient wilderness.

   _____

   _____

4. Our guide told us not to walk on the ice because it could be thin.

   _____

   _____

Name _____ Date _____

Focus Trait: Elaboration

Good writing is based on good ideas. You can express your ideas more vividly with figurative language. Similes, metaphors, and personification can help make your ideas come alive for a reader.

Simile The iceberg crackled and popped like a fire.

Metaphor The Arctic is an adventure waiting to happen.

Personification The gulls chattered about the events of the day.

Rewrite each of the following sentences to use figurative language.

Idea	Figurative Language to Use	New Sentence
The seal made its way into the water.	simile	
The arctic fox chased its prey.	simile	
There were migratory birds as far as the eye could see.	metaphor	
The sky was blue and looked very peaceful.	metaphor	
The tree looked old and broken.	personification	
There were many walruses on the icy shore.	personification	

 Reader's Guide

Vanishing Act

Write a Science Report

Tia is investigating some missing bees for her science project.
Use evidence from the text to complete her report. Remember
to write it from Tia's point of view.

Vanishing Act: The Mystery of the Disappearing Honeybees by Tia

Read page 37 to find out why the bees are important.

Introduction: _____

_____

_____

_____

Read page 37 to find out what problem Tia is investigating.

Problem/Purpose: _____

_____

_____

_____

Read the first two paragraphs on page 38 and the first paragraph on page 41 to find some of the possible causes Tia considered.

Possible Causes: _____

_____

_____

_____

Suppose that Tia presented her project at a science fair where people might ask her questions about her project. Help her answer the questions posed.

Read the first paragraph on page 41 and the map.

"I see that this was a problem on your friend's farm, but is the problem bigger than that?"

_____

_____

_____

Read the second paragraph on page 41.

"Hmmmm… you did not find a reason for the disappearance. Do you have any theories?"

_____

_____

_____

Review pages 36 and 37.

"What's the big deal? Less bees means less bee stings, right?"

_____

_____

_____

Latin Word Roots

Basic Write the Basic Word that best completes each group.

1. loud, noisy, _____

2. remove, take out, _____

3. put in, include, _____

4. order, recommend, _____

5. plan, suggestion, _____

6. force, order, _____

7. movement, advancement, _____

8. complaint, protest, _____

9. shorten, compress, _____

10. by hand, hand-operated, _____

11. tryout, test, _____

Challenge   You are a sculptor who draws your design on paper before you start working with your materials, which might include clay, wood, wire, or metal. Write a paragraph describing your process. Use at least three of the Challenge Words. Write on a separate sheet of paper.

Spelling Words

1. prescribe
2. contract
3. manufacture
4. progression
5. vocal
6. manual
7. audience
8. eject
9. impose
10. management
11. Congress
12. expose
13. inject
14. audition
15. manuscript
16. vocabulary
17. objection
18. manicure
19. proposal
20. extract

Challenge

manipulate
protractor
inscription
auditory
advocate

Grade 6, Unit 6

Spelling Word Sort

Write each Basic Word beside the correct heading. One Basic Word belongs in two groups.

Words with *scrib, script*	
Words with *tract*	
Words with *man*	
Words with *gress*	
Words with *voc*	
Words with *aud*	
Words with *ject*	
Words with *pos*	

Spelling Words

1. prescribe
2. contract
3. manufacture
4. progression
5. vocal
6. manual
7. audience
8. eject
9. impose
10. management
11. Congress
12. expose
13. inject
14. audition
15. manuscript
16. vocabulary
17. objection
18. manicure
19. proposal
20. extract

Challenge
manipulate
protractor
inscription
auditory
advocate

Challenge   Add the Challenge Words to your Word Sort.

Proofreading for Spelling

Find the misspelled words and circle them. Write them correctly on the lines below.

I saw a good documentary last night showing the progresion of how a television show goes from an idea to an actual program. First, a writer prepared a praposal describing the big idea for the show. Once managment approved the idea and signed a conrtact, writers got to work on preparing a script for a trial episode. Many writers got an opportunity to enject their ideas into the script. Sometimes a writer would raise a vocul ubjection to an idea or a word choice and argue to extrackt it from the story. Later, the producers would hold an auddition for actors. The pilot episode was taped in front of a live audeince. The pilot show was well received, but it did exposse some problems, causing the producers to inpose their ideas to improve the show. Finally, the show was ready to go into production and air on television!

Spelling Words

1. prescribe
2. contract
3. manufacture
4. progression
5. vocal
6. manual
7. audience
8. eject
9. impose
10. management
11. Congress
12. expose
13. inject
14. audition
15. manuscript
16. vocabulary
17. objection
18. manicure
19. proposal
20. extract

1. _____ 7. _____
2. _____ 8. _____
3. _____ 9. _____
4. _____ 10. _____
5. _____ 11. _____
6. _____ 12. _____

Commas with Introductory Words and Phrases

Use commas after introductory words and phrases.

- Set off introductory words such as *well*, *yes*, and *no* with a comma.

> **Yes,** I'd like to be part of the project.

- Set off long introductory prepositional phrases with a comma.

> **With a dramatic sigh,** Justin explained the problem.

- Use a comma after participial phrases that begin a sentence.

> **Buzzing from blossom to blossom,** the bees transfer pollen.

> **Thinking Question**
> *Is the meaning of the sentence clearer with a pause after the introductory word or phrase?*

Activity Rewrite each sentence. Add commas where they are needed.

1. When visiting Texas did you have time to see any farms?

   _____

2. Settling on a flower the bee began its search for nectar.

   _____

3. No bees do not usually sting beekeepers.

   _____

4. Mystified by the honeybee deaths scientists began an investigation.

   _____

5. Indeed a virus may be to blame for the honeybee crisis.

   _____

Commas in a Series

Commas should be used to separate three or more words or phrases in a series.

I want a book, a glass of water, and a quiet place to sit.

Commas can be used to combine sentences that tell about the same thing.

Multiple Sentences	Combined Sentence
John bought grapes. John bought apples. John bought pears.	John bought grapes, apples, and pears.

Thinking Question
How can these sentences be combined into one sentence?

Activity Write a new sentence combining each set of sentences.

1. The beekeeper bought a mask. The beekeeper bought gloves. The beekeeper bought a feeder.

   _____

2. The bees made honey. The bees stored honey. The bees then ate honey.

   _____

3. The queen bee buzzed. The queen bee flew around the hive. The queen bee landed.

   _____

4. The worker bees' lives are frantic. The worker bees' lives are nonstop. The worker bees' lives are short.

   _____

5. The bees cleaned the hive. The bees filled the hive. The bees lived in the hive.

   _____

Commas with Appositives

An **appositive** is a nonrestrictive word or phrase placed after a noun to identify or explain it. Use commas to separate an appositive from the rest of the sentence.

The worker bee, **a tireless worker**, lives a shorter life than the queen.

Thinking Questions
Is there a word or phrase placed after a noun to describe it? If so, how should it be punctuated?

1–4.   Rewrite each sentence.   Add commas where they are needed.

1. The queen bee the mother of the hive can produce more than 1,500 eggs a day.

_____

_____

2. The eggs all 1,500 of them will be incubated.

_____

3. The drones the only males in the colony have one job.

_____

4. The workers always busy keep the hive going.

_____

5–10.   Read the following paragraph.   Add commas where they are needed.

The work in a hive at least most of it is done by worker bees females that cannot reproduce. Young worker bees build the honeycomb a mass of cells and clean and guard the hive. They feed the queen and larvae with honey a thickened form of nectar. They control the temperature in the hive and carry out many other tasks. These are just a few of the tasks of the worker.

Correct Adjectives

Adjectives	How to Use	Examples
Articles	place before noun or another adjective: *a/an* refer to any one item; *the* refers to a specific item	We played **a** game. We shared **an** apple. **The** afternoon passed quickly.
Demonstratives	tell which one: *this, these* describe nearby objects; *that, those* describe distant objects	**This** bee is larger than **that** one. **These** hives need to be moved over by **those** trees.
Proper adjectives	formed from a proper noun: *Britain/British, Italy/Italian, China/Chinese*	Hornets swarmed around our **Italian** gelato and **British** scones.
Combining Sentences with Adjectives	Add endings *-y, -ed, -ing* to change other parts of speech to adjectives: *shine/shiny, frost/frosted, excite/exciting*	The windows were **frosted** with **shiny** crystal designs. The storm made the morning **exciting**.

1–4. Underline the correct word or words in parentheses to complete each sentence.

  1. If honeybees don't pollinate plants, (that, those) plants won't reproduce.

  2. Take (a, an, the) look at the hives.

  3. (These, Those) clouds on the horizon look threatening.

  4. (A, An) colony of honeybees is (a, an) incredible center of activity.

5–6. Combine details in each set of sentences to make a single sentence. Use proper adjectives when appropriate.

  5. Honeybees are brown or black. They have yellow stripes on their abdomens. They are insects.

  _____

  _____

  6. Some honeybees are from Africa. They are smaller than honeybees from Europe.

  _____

  _____

Connect to Writing

Choppy Sentences	Sentences Combined with Appositive
Colony foragers collect nectar from millions of flowers. Foragers are adult worker bees.	Colony foragers, adult worker bees, collect nectar from millions of flowers.

Activity Combine each set of sentences by using appositives.

1. A colony consists of a queen, some drones, and many thousands of worker bees. The colony is the social unit of the honeybee.

   _____

   _____

2. Drones live only about eight weeks. Drones are male bees.

   _____

   _____

3. The honeybee produces honey and beeswax. The honeybee is one of our oldest insect friends.

   _____

   _____

4. The old queen leaves with a group of bees, and a daughter queen inherits the hive. The daughter queen is the new ruler of the established colony.

   _____

   _____

Focus Trait: Elaboration

Narrative radio scripts can be written with all kinds of voices. It is important to match your voice to the content of the story.

Serious voice: Bearded dragons are omnivorous and eat both insects and plants.

Humorous voice: When ordering off the menu, bearded dragons often choose crickets with a side salad.

Read the radio script below. What makes it sound so serious? Rewrite it in your humorous voice.

Serious Voice

Narrator: Crickets can make your city apartment sound like a country night. Crickets are the favorite food of my pet bearded lizard, Frank. Because my mother tired of making continual trips to the pet store to buy them, we placed a large online order of crickets and kept them in an old, screen-covered fish tank. Of course, a few escaped. I suggested to my mother that we allow Frank to catch them, but she disagreed. After several hours, I thought we had completed our task. However, late that night, the crickets started chirping. I told my mother I thought our apartment sounded just like living in the country.

Humorous Voice

Narrator: _____

_____

_____

_____

_____

_____

_____

_____

Name _____ Date _____

Lesson 29
READER'S NOTEBOOK

Elephants on
the Savannah
Independent Reading

Elephants on the Savannah

Nature Journal

Write a nature journal about the observations made by Maya, Antonio, and Jordan. Use text evidence to complete the journal.

Reread page 51. Describe the observations. Include facts about the elephants.

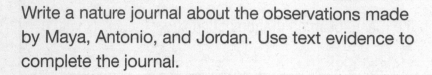

Kenya, East Africa
Morning Safari

_____
_____
_____
_____
_____

Reread pages 52–53. Suppose one of the elephants sensed danger. Use text evidence to record what might have been observed.

_____
_____
_____

Name _____ Date _____

Lesson 29
READER'S NOTEBOOK

**Elephants on
the Savannah**
Independent Reading

Reread page 55. Imagine that Maya recorded in the nature journal, "I used to think that animals did not have feelings, but after today I changed my mind." What might have changed her mind?

_____

_____

_____

_____

Reread page 56. Use the text and illustrations to draw a picture of what was observed. Include callouts and labels to give facts about the elephants.

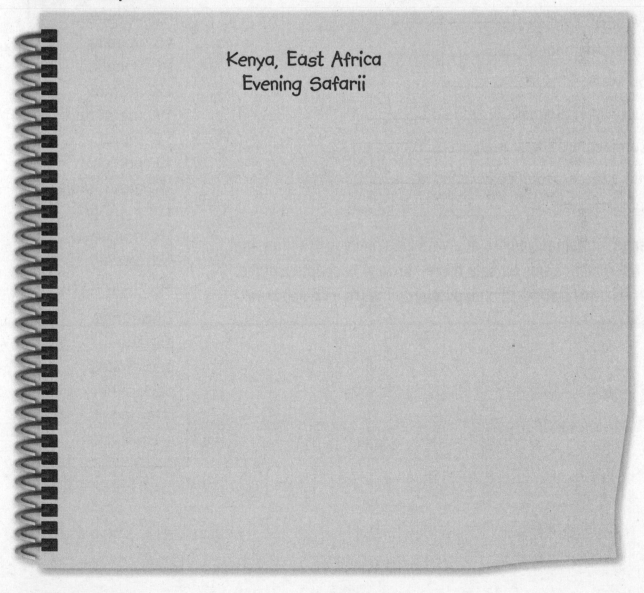

Kenya, East Africa
Evening Safarii

Greek and Latin Word Parts

Basic Write the Basic Word that best completes each group.

1. biography, journal, _____

2. handle, knob, _____

3. deadly, life-threatening, _____

4. sing, yell, _____

5. walker, hiker, _____

6. special, unforgettable, _____

7. doctor, orthodontist, _____

8. platform, stage, _____

9. trader, merchant, _____

10. job, work, _____

11. supervisor, director, _____

12. worm, caterpillar, _____

13. embarrassed, terrified, _____

14. singer, performer, _____

Challenge Imagine you are at a yard sale and you are browsing some interesting items for sale there. Write a description of the items. Use three of the Challenge Words. Write on a separate sheet of paper.

Spelling Words

1. pedal
2. peddler
3. pedestrian
4. pedestal
5. centipede
6. dental
7. dentist
8. dentures
9. vocalize
10. vocalist
11. vocation
12. memoir
13. memorial
14. tripod
15. podium
16. memorable
17. manager
18. manifest
19. mortal
20. mortified

Challenge
impede
pediatrician
pedometer
mannequin
memorabilia

Name _____ Date _____

Lesson 29
READER'S NOTEBOOK

Elephants on the
Savannah
Spelling: Greek and Latin
Word Parts

Spelling Word Sort

Write each Basic Word beside the correct heading.

Words with *ped* or *pod*	
Words with *dent*	
Words with *voc*	
Words with *mem*	
Words with *man*	
Words with *mort*	

Challenge   Add the Challenge Words to your Word Sort.

Spelling Words

1. pedal
2. peddler
3. pedestrian
4. pedestal
5. centipede
6. dental
7. dentist
8. dentures
9. vocalize
10. vocalist
11. vocation
12. memoir
13. memorial
14. tripod
15. podium
16. memorable
17. manager
18. manifest
19. mortal
20. mortified

Challenge
impede
pediatrician
pedometer
mannequin
memorabilia

Name _____ Date _____

Proofreading for Spelling

Find the misspelled words and circle them. Write them correctly on the lines below.

Myra stepped up to the podeum. She seemed morified as she looked around the room at her classmates. To vocalise her poem in front of a group was Myra's biggest fear. In order to pass speech class, though, she had to do it.

"What is your dream vocacion?" Myra choked out. Ms. Santos gave her an encouraging smile. Myra took a deep breath and continued. "If you want to fit dentchures for your great auntie, go to dentul school. A detnist is what you'll be. Should you write a memmoir, being an author might be more your thing. Or if you're a good voculist, perhaps you should sing! Maybe you'd like to be a mannager at a shop. Perhaps you'd like to help a podestian as a traffic cop. Whether you're a cenipede-handler at a zoo or a cook making stew, make your job memurable and fun for you." Shyly, Myra looked down as the class burst into applause.

Spelling Words

1. pedal
2. peddler
3. pedestrian
4. pedestal
5. centipede
6. dental
7. dentist
8. dentures
9. vocalize
10. vocalist
11. vocation
12. memoir
13. memorial
14. tripod
15. podium
16. memorable
17. manager
18. manifest
19. mortal
20. mortified

1. _____   8. _____

2. _____   9. _____

3. _____   10. _____

4. _____   11. _____

5. _____   12. _____

6. _____   13. _____

7. _____

Commas in Longer Sentences

- Use a **comma** to separate the simple sentences that make up a **compound sentence.** Place the comma before the conjunction.

    The African elephant is not the world's largest animal, **but** it is the largest land mammal.

- Use a comma to separate the parts of a complex sentence when the first part begins with a subordinating conjunction.

    Because most elephant behavior has to be learned, mother elephants keep their young with them for years.

Thinking Questions
Are there two simple sentences joined by a conjunction? Is there a complex sentence that begins with a subordinating conjunction?

Activity Rewrite each sentence. Add commas where they are needed.

1. An elephant's trunk is a versatile tool and the huge animal uses it constantly.

   _____

2. Elephants can run as fast as 25 mph but they cannot jump.

   _____

3. When danger threatens adult elephants form a circle around the young.

   _____

4. After the male calves reach maturity they leave the mother's herd.

   _____

5. Grown male elephants live alone or they travel in bachelor herds.

   _____

6. Because elephants were killed for their ivory elephant populations shrank quickly.

   _____

   _____

Other Uses for Commas

- When writing a letter, use a comma between the name of a city and state. In a sentence, use a comma after the state as well.

    Chicago, Illinois
    We flew to Chicago, Illinois, for the conference.

- Use a comma between the day and the year in a date. In a sentence, use a comma after the year as well.

    March 13, 2015
    On March 13, 2015, we will travel to the state conference.

Thinking Question
Are the city and state, or the day and year, written in a sentence?

Activity Rewrite each sentence. Add commas where they are needed.

1. "The Star-Spangled Banner" was written on the morning of September 14 1814 in Baltimore Maryland.

    _____

    _____

2. Before moving to Dallas Texas she lived in Tokyo Japan.

    _____

3. Abraham Lincoln was born on February 12 1809.

    _____

4. On May 25 2010 our class will go to the zoo in St. Louis Missouri.

    _____

Commas with Nouns of Direct Address

A **noun of direct address** is the name of a person who is spoken to directly. Use commas to set off nouns of direct address.

Is the matriarch larger than the other elephants in the herd**, Dad?**

Thinking Question
Is a person directly addressed in the sentence?

1–4.   Rewrite each sentence. Add commas where they are needed.

1. Jake did you know that elephants are mammals?

_____

2. For instance Sofia they actually have hair on their bodies.

_____

3. What do you think about elephants being used in circuses Mom?

_____

4. Dad what's your opinion on the subject?

_____

5–15.   Use proofreading marks to edit the following paragraph from a letter. Add commas where they are needed. Include quotation marks when necessary.

Wiley let's take a trip to Africa! There's so much to do there. For example Wiley we could go on a safari. I would love to see giraffes, lions, and hyenas. Wouldn't that be great? I asked Professor Jenkins all about it. I said Professor tell me what you saw on your trip. She said Gina I saw more elephants than you could imagine.

Making Comparisons

- **Adjectives** can be used to compare two or more people, places, or things.
- Add *-er* to form the **comparative** and *-est* to form the **superlative** of one-syllable adjectives and some two-syllable adjectives.
- Use *more* and *most* to compare many two-syllable adjectives and all adjectives with three or more syllables. Use *less* and *least* to compare adjectives of any length.

Adjectives	Comparative (compare 2)	Superlative (compare 3 or more)
large	larger	largest
honest	more honest	most honest
expensive	less expensive	least expensive

Activity Underline the correct word or words in parentheses to complete each sentence.

1. The elephant is the (larger, largest) land animal in the world.

2. Humans are the (bigger, biggest) threat to elephants.

3. Of the two elephants, that one was (bigger, biggest)

4. Between the elephant and the manatee, I thought the elephant was (more, most) impressive.

5. She is the (more, most) skilled animal trainer I have ever seen.

6. The manatee was (least, less) agile than the elephant.

Connect to Writing

Choppy, Repetitive Sentences	Smooth, Combined Sentences
Manatees are related to elephants. Both are herbivores. Elephants carry their young for many months. Manatees also carry their young for many months. Also, they have the same unique molars that elephants have.	Both manatees and elephants are herbivores, both carry their young for many months, and both have the same unique molars.

Activity Combine each set of sentences by writing them as one sentence. Use commas to separate items in a series.

1. During the Ice Age, the woolly mammoth grew larger. It became bulkier.

   It also grew a woolly fur coat.

   _____

   _____

2. Unlike today's elephant, the woolly mammoth had small ears. It had tusks that were

   longer and more curved. Also, it had thick brown fur, unlike today's elephant.

   _____

   _____

3. Elephants collect food with their trunks. They cool off by fanning their ears.

   Their tusks are used for fighting.

   _____

   _____

4. Elephants use their trunks for breathing. Elephants also use their trunks for

   drinking. The trunk also can be used to pick up large or small objects.

   _____

   _____

Name _____ Date _____

Lesson 29
READER'S NOTEBOOK

Elephants on the
Savannah
Writing: Narrative Writing

Focus Trait: Development
Showing Instead of Telling

Tells an Event or Emotion	Shows the Event or Emotion
I felt scared.	Fear raced through me, halting my breath and turning my knees to water.

Pair/Share Work with a partner to write examples that show each event or emotion.

Tells an Event or Emotion	Shows the Event or Emotion
I saw the elephants	
The elephants walked into the river.	
A baby elephant drank water.	
Then I saw the lion.	
I felt nervous.	
One elephant let the others know.	
The lion stopped and then left.	

 **Reader's Guide**

Storm Chasers

Nature Journal

Storm chasing is a risky and dangerous job. Think about the work storm chasers perform. Then use evidence from the text and illustrations to help you create a checklist to help the storm chasers prepare for a chase.

Reread pages 66 and 70 and complete the checklist.

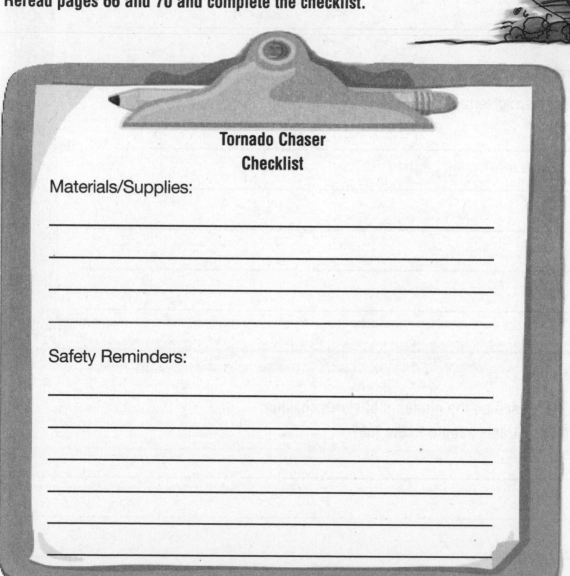

**Tornado Chaser
Checklist**

Materials/Supplies:

_____

_____

_____

_____

Safety Reminders:

_____

_____

_____

_____

_____

Reread pages 68 and 71 and complete the checklist.

**Hurricane Chaser
Checklist**

Materials/Supplies:

_____

_____

_____

Safety Reminders:

_____

_____

_____

_____

**Reread page 69. Based on the pioneers of storm chasing,
what do you think attracts people to the job?**

_____

_____

_____

394

Words Often Confused

Basic Complete the puzzle by writing the Basic Word for each clue.

Spelling Words

1. desert
2. dessert
3. hardy
4. hearty
5. moral
6. morale
7. laying
8. lying
9. personal
10. personnel
11. formally
12. formerly
13. healthy
14. healthful
15. precede
16. proceed
17. conscious
18. conscience
19. immigrate
20. emigrate

Challenge
sympathy
empathy
imminent
eminent

Across

4. a sense of what is right or wrong
6. to move into a new country
9. to move out of a country
10. people who work for an organization
11. good for you

Down

1. present participle of "lie"
2. robust, healthy, and satisfying
3. abandon
5. to move forward
7. a strong belief
8. to come before

Challenge You are an advice columnist for your school newspaper. Write an answer to someone who has a problem. Use three Challenge Words. Write on a separate sheet of paper.

Spelling Word Sort

Write each Basic Word beside the correct heading.

Often confused verb pairs	
Often confused adjective pairs	
Other often confused pairs	

Challenge Add the Challenge Words to your Word Sort.

Spelling Words

1. desert
2. dessert
3. hardy
4. hearty
5. moral
6. morale
7. laying
8. lying
9. personal
10. personnel
11. formally
12. formerly
13. healthy
14. healthful
15. precede
16. proceed
17. conscious
18. conscience
19. immigrate
20. emigrate

Challenge
sympathy
empathy
imminent
eminent

Proofreading for Spelling

Storm Chasers
Spelling: Words Often Confused

**Find the misspelled or incorrectly used words and circle them.
Write them correctly on the lines below.**

For centuries, we have assumed that the oceans were too heardy to actually be harmed by our everyday activities. However, we need to alter this misguided thinking. Scientists have formaly challenged governments to address the problem. For those who were formelry uninterested in this issue, the desire to maintain healthful oceans should now be a matter of personel conscence. After all, the seas are all connected. We cannot emegrate to a new, clean planet. For many years, environmental groups have been lying the groundwork for international cooperation. Now that people all around the world are trying to work together, the morral of ecologists is high and it is time to precede. The morul we must learn is: We have the power to improve the environment, if we all make a conschious effort to help.

Spelling Words

1. desert
2. dessert
3. hardy
4. hearty
5. moral
6. morale
7. laying
8. lying
9. personal
10. personnel
11. formally
12. formerly
13. healthy
14. healthful
15. precede
16. proceed
17. conscious
18. conscience
19. immigrate
20. emigrate

1. _____   7. _____

2. _____   8. _____

3. _____   9. _____

4. _____   10. _____

5. _____   11. _____

6. _____   12. _____

Semicolons

A **semicolon** should be used between the two independent clauses of a compound sentence when there is no coordinating conjunction.

> The clouds covered the sky; it was dark suddenly.

Semicolons can also be used to separate items. If items in a list already have punctuation inside of them, **semicolons** can be used to separate the items and to make things clearer.

> The new students were Gabe from Johnson City, Tennessee; Linda from Chicago, Illinois; and Eric from San Francisco, California.

Thinking Question
What should be used to join two independent clauses without a coordinating conjunction?

Activity Combine related sentences using a semicolon. If the sentences are not related, write "no semicolon."

1. The sky was growing cloudy. It looked gray and threatening.

   _____

   _____

2. We saw the storm clouds approaching. They were moving fast.

   _____

   _____

3. The weather report on TV was wrong. Well, at least I got to stay home from school.

   _____

4. I had time on my hands. I had to think of something to do.

   _____

   _____

5. I thought about watching a movie. I found one about storm chasers.

   _____

   _____

Colons

Use a **colon** to introduce a list, to show time of day, and after the greeting in a formal business letter.

The weather is broadcast at **5:15** P.M. and **6:15** P.M.

Tornadoes occur often in the following states: Kansas, Oklahoma, and Missouri.

Dear Ms. Johnson:
Please add my name to your mailing list.

Thinking Questions
Does the sentence formally introduce a list? Does it include the time of day? Is it the greeting of a formal business inquiry?

1–4. **Rewrite each sentence, adding colons as needed.**

1. We keep the following emergency supplies in the basement a flashlight, food, water, and blankets.

_____

_____

2. The storm struck the coast at 230 A.M.

_____

3. The following storms can be very dangerous tornadoes, hurricanes, and blizzards.

_____

_____

4. Dear Mr. Petros
Thank you for your inquiry.

_____

Using Parentheses

Parentheses are used to set off **parenthetical elements**, such as examples, explanations, or supplementary facts. This material is added to a sentence but is not vital to its meaning.

Storm spotters (called Sky Hawks) are always watching the sky for storm clouds.

Thinking Question
If the information in parentheses was removed, would the sentence still have its complete meaning?

Activity Rewrite each sentence. Add parentheses where they are needed.

1. The encyclopedia Volume 10 has a very informative article about tornadoes.

   _____

   _____

2. The National Weather Service NWS offers updated weather warnings for each state.

   _____

   _____

3. The 1900 Galveston hurricane September 8, 1900 was a catastrophe for the Gulf Coast.

   _____

   _____

4. FEMA Federal Emergency Management Agency offers assistance for large-scale disasters

   _____

   _____

More Comparisons

Some adverbs have irregular forms of comparison.

Irregular Adverb	Comparative (compare 2)	Superlative (compare 3 or more)
The cleanup went **well**.	The cleanup could have gone **better**.	Yesterday's cleanup went **best** of any we have done.
Our town fared **badly** in the storm.	Johnson City fared **worse** than we did.	Monroe fared **worst** of all communities.
Jan studies the weather **little**.	Brian studies the weather **less** than Jan.	Mike studies the weather **least** of all.
The wind doesn't blow **much** here.	The wind blows **more** in the plains.	It blows **most** in the city of Chicago.

1–6.   Underline the correct form of the adverb in each sentence.

1. Damaging storms occurred (much, more, most) frequently in 2008 than in 2007.

2. Tornadoes occur (much, more, most) often in spring and summer.

3. The big storm scared our cat (little, less, least) than our dog.

4. Storms frighten our dog, Patches, (much, more, most) of all when she cannot find a place to hide.

5. Does it snow (much, more, most) in Arkansas?

6. It snows (much, more, most) in Arkansas than in Florida.

7–10.   Rewrite the paragraph. Use the correct form of the adverb in parentheses in each sentence.

Which kind of storm do people dread (much) of all? Blizzards shut down travel (much) effectively than tornadoes. People can often prepare (well) for hurricanes than tornadoes, but tornadoes damage things (badly).

_____

_____

_____

Connect to Writing

Sentence with Errors	Corrected Sentence
Connie's report covered the following topics conditions for storms and preparing for storms.	Connie's report covered the following topics: conditions for storms and preparing for storms.

Sentence with Errors	Corrected Sentence
The weather map Chart B accurately tracked the storm.	The weather map (Chart B) accurately tracked the storm.

Activity Find the errors in punctuation in each sentence. Rewrite each sentence correctly.

1. The National Oceanic and Atmospheric Administration NOAA predicted a catastrophic storm.

   _____

   _____

2. The following facts are important Earth's atmosphere is growing warmer, polar ice is melting, and unstable air masses appear to be causing more destructive storms.

   _____

   _____

   _____

3. Dear Mr. Hilleson
   Enclosed you will find the following items a check for $350, directions for continuing disaster relief, and contact information.

   _____

   _____

   _____

Focus Trait: Organization

Grouping ideas into paragraphs and maintaining time order is an important skill. Read the sentences below. Rewrite them in a paragraph that makes sense.

Ideas

- Only the next few seconds would tell.
- The wind grew to a roar, and I watched a funnel cloud approach
- Branches from trees snapped off at the trunks.
- The day started out as beautiful but rapidly changed into a terror.
- Would it hit our house?
- My bicycle went skidding across the driveway.
- The sky grew dark, and the wind began to blow.
- It was the fifth of April, and I had just turned 14 years old.

Ideas Organized into Logical Order in a Paragraph

_____

_____

_____

_____

_____

_____

_____